Social-Emotional Learning Activities

For The Elementary Grades

Introduction and Theory by
Dianne Schilling

Contributing Authors

**Terri Akin • David Cowan • Gerry Dunne
Susanna Palomares • Dianne Schilling
Sandy Schuster • Eden Steele**

INNERCHOICE Publishing

INNERCHOICE Publishing
15079 Oak Chase Court
Wellington, FL 33414

www.InnerchoicePublishing.com

Contents

Introduction

This activity guide is a collection of the most popular and effective social and emotional learning activities offered by Innerchoice Publishing. Over the years, Innerchoice Publishing has developed dozens of activity guides which have been used in thousands of schools throughout the country. Many of these books have been translated and used sucessfully in other countries interested in developing the emotional and social aspects of students lives. You are invited to use this newest contribution to the SEL curricular mosaic as:

• the core of your SEL curriculum
• a specialized SEL supplement to your existing curriculum

This book provides relevant student friendly activities for classroom and counseling groups. For optimum impact SEL is not a single program or group of activities but a coordinated framework across classrooms, counseling groups, homes, communities and districts.

The bottom line is, don't neglect or take for granted the emotional life of your students. Feelings, self-awareness, life skills, conflict management, self-esteem, and all of the other developmental areas now identified as social emotional learning are critically important. An impressive array of research from multiple fields supports the validity of time and energy spent by educators in these domains. Emotions are not unruly remnants of stone-age survival to be hushed and otherwise ignored while we develop cognitive skills. Emotions drive our behavior, shape our values, and predispose us to choose one course of action over others. Emotional and rational skills are equally important interdependent components of human intelligence.

Unit Organization

The five units in this guide each contain group activities, Sharing Circles, individual experience sheets, and comprise a complete SEL curriculum. They are:

• Self-awareness

Building a vocabulary for feelings, knowing the likes, dislikes, hopes, preferences, talents, shortcomings, and other uniquenesses that make up the individual. Becoming aware of inner and outer states and processes. Establishing a firm sense of identity and feeling esteem and acceptance of oneself; monitoring "self-talk" to catch negative messages such as internal put-downs; acknowledging the talents and abilities of self and others.

• Self-Management

Knowing the relationship between thoughts, feelings and actions; accurately reading feeling cues in others and responding appropriately; realizing what is behind feelings (e.g. the primary feelings underlying anger) and learning how to constructively express and control feelings. Understanding what stress is, where it comes from, and how it affects daily living; learning to use exercise, guided imagery, relaxation methods, and attitude changes to control and relieve stress.

• Social Awareness

Taking the perspective and understanding the feelings of others; developing caring and compassionate attitudes. Working self-reflectively in groups while monitoring behaviors and roles; practicing cooperation and interdependence.

• Relationship Skills

Learning and practicing effective communication skills; listening actively; and, engaging in effective two-way communication using good listening and speaking skills. Understanding that conflict is normal and potentially productive; learning how to fight fair with others; learning and practicing a variety of conflict-resolution strategies.

• Responsible Decision Making

Examining what goes into making decisions; considering actions and knowing their consequence; recognizing the existence of personal choice in almost all situations; taking responsibility for decisions and actions.

Each of these units contains eight to ten group activities and six fully developed Sharing Circles, along with a list of additional Sharing Circle topics, which allow you to repeat the impact of the powerful circle process for many weeks. Before you lead your first Sharing Circle, be sure to read the section, "How to Conduct A Sharing Circle" on page 15.

Many of the activities include handouts, called "Experience Sheets," for you to duplicate and distribute to students. Experience sheets are written in a conversational style and speak directly to the individual student. Directions for their use are imbedded in the printed procedure for leading each activity.

The units are arranged in a suggested order, but may be implemented with considerable flexibility. We encourage you to maintain an agile, expansive attitude as you move through (or skip among) the units. Allow the reactions of students to spark new ideas for strengthening social and emotional skills in each topic area.

Finally, please make any adjustments necessary to accommodate the interests, abilities, cultural backgrounds and learning styles of your students. Your experience and regular contact with students put you in an ideal position to interpret signals regarding relevancy and modify the activities accordingly.

The Impact of Social and Emotional Learning

Emotions impact every area of life: health, learning, behavior, and relationships.

Children and young people who are emotionally competent— who manage their own feelings well, and who recognize and respond effectively to the feelings of others — are at an advantage in every area of life, whether family and peer relationships, school, sports, or community and organizational pursuits. Children with well-developed emotional skills are also more likely to lead happy and productive lives, and to master the habits of mind that will assure them personal and career success as adults.

In homes and schools where social and emotional learning is nurtured, children tolerate frustration better, get into fewer fights, and engage in less self-destructive behavior. They are healthier, less lonely, less impulsive, and more focused. Human relationships improve, and so does academic achievement.

Health

There is no longer any question that emotions can profoundly affect health. Science used to believe that the brain and nervous system were separate and distinct from the immune system. In fact, the two systems are in close communication, sending messages back and forth continuously. Furthermore, chemical messengers which operate in both the brain and the immune system are concentrated *most heavily* in neural areas that regulate emotion.

Numerous studies have shown that positive, supportive relationships are good medicine, bolstering immune function, speeding recovery time, and prolonging life. The prognosis for people in ill health who have caring family and friends is dramatically better than for people without emotional support.

Learning

Almost all students who do poorly in school lack one or more elements of emotional intelligence. Study after study has shown that competence in emotional skills results not only in higher academic achievement on the part of students, but in significantly more instructional time on the part of teachers. Emotionally competent children are far less disruptive and require fewer disciplinary interventions.

Recent research has shown impressive benefits for students who participate in SEL programs. A meta-analysis published in the journal Child Development showed an 11 percentile gain in academic achievement. A study published in the Journal of Benefit-Cost Analysis, conducted by economist Clive Belfield and colleagues at Teachers College, Columbia University, demonstrated a roughly $11 benefit for every $1 spent on rigorous SEL programing.

Children who are emotionally competent have an increased desire to learn and to achieve, both within school and without. Positive emotions — excitement, curiosity, pride — are the fuel that drives motivation. Passion moves young people toward their goals.

Behavior

Violence and disorder in America's schools have reached crisis proportions. Teachers who once dealt with mischievous, unruly students and an occasional temper tantrum are now demanding emergency phones in their classrooms, security guards in the hallways, and metal detectors at the gates. As long as such conditions continue, all education suffers. Rates of teen suicide, pregnancy, and drug abuse testify to the need for emotional literacy: self-awareness, decision-making, self-confidence, and stress management.

Relationships

Children who are effective in social interactions are capable of understanding their peers. They know how to interact with other children and adults — flexibly, skillfully, and responsibly — without sacrificing their own needs and integrity. They have a good sense of timing and are effective at being heard and getting help when they need it. Socially competent children can process the nonverbal as well as verbal messages of others, and recognize that the behaviors of one person can affect another. They take responsibility for their actions.

Children who cannot interpret or express emotions feel frustrated. They don't understand what's going on around them. They are frequently viewed as strange, and cause others to feel uncomfortable. Without social competence, children can easily misinterpret a look or statement and respond inappropriately, yet lack the ability to express their uncertainty or clarify the intentions and desires of others. They may lack empathy and be relatively unaware of how their behavior affects others.

Controlling Emotions

The ability to bring out-of-control emotions back into line results in what our parents and grandparents called emotional maturity. Present terminology labels it emotional competence, or self-management the "master aptitude."

Self-Awareness

The first step in getting children to control their emotional responses is to help them develop self-awareness. Through self-awareness, children learn to give ongoing attention to their internal states, to know what they are feeling when they are feeling it, to identify the events that precipitate upsets and emotional hijackings, and to bring their feelings back under control.

Self-awareness allows children to manage their feelings and to recover from bad moods more quickly. Children who are self-aware don't hide things from themselves. Labeling feelings makes them their own. They can talk about fear, frustration, excitement, and envy and they can understand and speculate concerning such feelings in others, too.

Lacking self-awareness, children may become engulfed by their feelings, lost in them, overwhelmed by them. Unawareness of what is going on in their inner and outer worlds sets the stage for lack of congruence between what they believe or feel and how they behave. Feelings of isolation ("I'm the only one who feels this way.") occur when children are unaware that others experience the same range of feelings that they do. Without self-awareness children never gain control over their lives. By default, their courses are plotted by others or by parts of themselves which they fail to recognize.

Self-awareness can take the form of nonjudgmental observation ("I'm feeling irritated.") or it can be accompanied by evaluative thoughts ("I shouldn't feel this way" or "Don't think about that.") Although in and of themselves, emotions are neither right nor wrong, good nor bad, these kinds of judgments are common and indicate that the neocortical circuits are monitoring the emotion. However, to try to abolish a feeling or attempt to take away a feeling in someone else only drives the emotion out of awareness, where its activity along neural pathways continues unmonitored and unabated — as neuroses, insomnia, ulcers, and communication failures of all kinds testify.

Managing Anger and Curbing Impulses

Contrary to what many of us used to believe, when it comes to anger "letting it all out" is *not* helpful. Acting on anger will generally make a child angrier, and each angry outburst will prolong and deepen the distress.

What does work is to teach children to keep a lid on their feelings while they buy some time. If children wait until they have cooled down, they can confront the other person calmly. When flooded with negative emotions the ability to hear, think, and speak are severely impaired. Taking a "time out" can be enormously constructive. However 5 minutes is not enough; research suggests that people need at least 20 minutes to recover from intense physiological arousal.

Research has also shown quite conclusively that it's possible for a child to keep an angry mood going (and growing) just by thinking (and talking) about it.

The longer a child dwells on what made her angry, the more reasons and self-justifications she can find for being angry. So when encouraging children to talk about their feelings, we need to be careful not to fan the flames.

Brooding fuels anger, but seeing things differently quells it. Reframing a situation is one of the most potent ways of controlling emotions.

Sadness: Shifting Gears

Depression and sadness are low-arousal states. When a child is sad, it's as though a master gauge has turned down everything: mouth, eyes, head, shoulders, speech, energy, motivation, desire. Taking a jog is probably the last thing the child feels like doing, but by forcing himself out the door and down the path, he will experience a lift.

The key seems to be shifting the mind from a low-arousal state to a high-arousal state. Exercise and positive distracting activities, like seeing a funny movie, turn up the master gauge, relieving sadness, melancholy, and mild depression. Another way to accomplish the shift is to engineer a small success, such as improving a skill, winning a game, or completing a project.

Humor is great at lifting children out of the doldrums and can add significantly to their creativity and ability to solve problems, too. In studies documenting the effects of humor, people were able to think more broadly, associate more freely, and generate more creative solutions and decisions after hearing a joke.

The ability of humor to boost creativity and improve decision making stems from the fact that memory is "state specific." When we're in a good mood, we come up with more positive solutions and decisions. When we're in a bad mood, the alternatives we generate reflect our negativity.

Choosing to watch cartoons, shoot baskets, ride a bike, or spend a few minutes on the computer is a decision that the rational mind can take. The emotional mind can't be stopped from generating sadness and melancholy, but children can learn to tap into strategies that lead them out of the gloom.

Relationship Skills

If they are fortunate, children are surrounded by people who give them attention, are actively involved in their lives, and model healthy, responsible interpersonal behavior. Core skills in the art of relationships are empathy, listening, mastery of nonverbal cues, and the ability to manage the emotions of others — to make accurate interpretations, respond appropriately, work cooperatively, and resolve conflicts.

Howard Gardner's theory of multiple intelligence includes two personal intelligences, *interpersonal* and *intrapersonal*. People with high interpersonal intelligence have the capacity to discern and respond appropriately to the moods, temperaments, motivations, and desires of others. Intrapersonal intelligence gives people ready access to their own feeling life, the ability to discriminate among their emotions, and accurate awareness of their strengths and weaknesses.

The personal intelligences equip children to monitor their own expressions of emotion, attune to the ways others react, fine-tune their social performance to have the desired effect, express unspoken collective sentiments and guide groups toward goals. Personal intelligence is the basis of leadership.

Lacking personal intelligence, young people are apt to make poor choices related to such important decisions as who to befriend, emulate, date, and marry, what skills to develop and what career to pursue.

Empathy. All social skills are built on a base of emotional attunement, on the capacity for empathy. The ability to "walk in another's moccasins" is the foundation of caring and altruism. Violent people lack empathy.

Empathy is an outgrowth of self-awareness. The more we are able to understand our own emotions, the more skilled we are at understanding and responding to the emotions of others. Empathy plays heavily in making moral judgments. Sharing their pain, fear, or neglect is what moves us to help people in distress. Putting ourselves in the place of others motivates us to follow moral principles — to treat others the way we want to be treated.

These abilities have little to do with rational intelligence. Studies have shown that students with high levels of empathy are among the most popular, well adjusted, and high performing students, yet their IQs are no higher than those of students who are less skilled at reading nonverbal cues.

Empathy begins to develop very early in life. When infants and children under two witness the upset of another child, they react as if the distress were their own. Seeing another child cry is likely to bring them to tears and send them to a parent's arms.

From about the age of two on, when children begin to grasp the concept of their own separateness, they typically seek to console a distressed child by giving toys, petting, or hugging. In late childhood, they are able to view distress as an outgrowth of a person's condition or station in life. At this stage of development, children are capable of empathizing with entire groups such as the poor, the homeless, and victims of war.

Empathy can be developed through various forms of perspective-taking. In conflict situations, children can be asked to listen to each other's feelings and point of view, and then to feed back or summarize the opposing perspective. Imagining the feelings of characters in literature as well as figures from current events and history is also effective. Combining role playing with these strategies makes them even more powerful.

Nonverbal Communication Skills. The mode of communication used by the rational mind is words; the mode preferred by the emotional mind is nonverbal. We telegraph and receive excitement, happiness, sorrow, anger, and all the other emotions through facial expressions and body movements. When words contradict these nonverbal messages — "I'm fine," hissed through clenched teeth — nine times out of ten we can believe the nonverbal and discount the verbal.

Acting out various feelings teaches children to be more aware of nonverbal behavior, as does identifying feelings from videos, photos, and illustrations.

Emotions are contagious and transferrable. When two children interact, the more emotionally expressive of the pair readily transfers feelings to the more passive. Again, this transfer is accomplished *nonverbally.*

Children with high levels of emotional intelligence are able to attune to other children's (and adult's) moods and bring others under the sway of their own feelings, setting the emotional tone of an interaction.

Guided by cultural background, children learn certain display rules concerning the expression of emotions, such as minimizing or exaggerating particular feelings, or substituting one feeling for another, as when a child displays confidence while feeling confused. As educators in a multiethnic, multiracial society, we need to be sensitive to a variety of cultural display rules, and help students gain a similar awareness.

Listening. Through listening, children learn empathy, gather information, develop cooperative relationships, and build trust. Skillful listening is required for engaging in conversations and discussions, negotiating agreements, resolving conflicts and many other emotional and cognitive competencies.

Few skills have greater and more lasting value than listening. Unfortunately, listening skills are generally learned by happenstance, not by direct effort. The vast majority of children and adults are either unable or unwilling to listen attentively and at length to another person.

Research shows that poor listening impedes learning and destroys comprehension. However, when students are taught to listen effectively, both comprehension and academic performance go up, along with classroom cooperation and self-esteem. Listening facilitates both emotional learning and academic learning.

Conflict Management. Schools are rife with opportunities for conflict. From the farthest reaches of the playground to the most remote corners of the classroom, from student restrooms to the teacher's lounge, a thousand little things each day create discord. The causes are many.

Children bring to school an accumulation of everything they've learned — all of their habits and all the beliefs they've developed about themselves, other people, and their world. Such diversity makes conflict inevitable. And because the conflict-resolution skills of most children are poorly developed, the outcomes of conflict are frequently negative — at times even destructive.

Diversity also breeds conflict. Learning to understand, respect and appreciate similarities and differences is one key to resolving conflicts. Unfortunately most of us learn as children that there is only one right answer. From the moment this fallacious notion receives acceptance, the mind closes and vision narrows.

Prejudice cannot be eliminated, but the emotional learning underlying prejudice can be *relearned*. One way to accomplish relearning is to engineer projects and activities in which diverse groups work together to obtain common goals. Social cliques, particularly hostile ones, intensify negative stereotypes. But when children work together as equals to attain a common goal — on committees, sports teams, performing groups — stereotypes break down.

 Peer mediation programs offer another excellent avenue for relearning ineffective emotional responses to conflict. Mediators act as models, facilitators and coaches, helping their classmates develop listening, conflict resolution, and problem-solving skills.

Educating the Emotional Brain

Social and Emotional skills are core competencies. To raise the level of these skills in students, schools need to focus more on the emotional aspects of children's lives, which are often ignored.

Unfortunately, in classes that stress subject-matter mastery, teaching is often devoid of emotional content. Too many educators believe that if somehow students master school subjects, they will be well prepared for life. Such a view suffers from a shallow and distorted understanding of how the human brain functions.

Many of the competencies that should be addressed by educational programs in SEL have been specified on the previous pages. A number of outlines are suggested by Daniel Goleman in his book, *Emotional Intelligence.* One of the most useful comes from Peter Salovey, a former Yale psychologist and current President of Yale University, whose list of emotional competencies includes a set of four abilities: Perceiving emotions, using emotions, understanding emotions, and managing emotions.

The Collaborative for Academic, Social, and Emotional Learning (CASEL)has identified Five social and emotional competencies: Self-awarenwss, Self-management, Social Awareness, Relationship Skills, and Responsible Decision Making. This book has utulized these competencies in it's chapter organization.

To be most effective, SEL content and processes should be applied consistently across the curriculum and at all grade levels. Children should be afforded many opportunities for skill practice, through a combination of dedicated activities and the countless unplanned "teachable moments" that occur daily. When emotional lessons are repeated over and over, they are reflected in strengthened neural pathways in the brain. They become positive habits that surface in times of stress.

Weaving EQ Into the Curriculum

Teachers may resist the idea of adding new content areas to the curriculum. In most cases, demands on teacher time are already at or beyond the saturation point, but this needn't be an insurmountable obstacle to emotional education. Feelings are part of everything that children do, and they can be part of everything they learn, too.

By incorporating lessons in social and emotional learning within traditional subject areas, we assist students to grasp the connections between realms of academic knowledge and life experience, and encourage them to utilize their multiple intelligences. This approach fits well with the concept of multidisciplinary teaching.

When a curriculum adheres to traditional straight and narrow subject areas and is devoid of emotional content, the subject matter is unlikely to "live" for students because of the curriculum's cold and reductionistic nature. With the world growing more complex by the minute, such an approach makes it extremely difficult for children to integrate the parts and pieces of what they learn, much less apply them within a real-world context.

By suggesting relationships and posing the right questions, by being observant and noticing nonverbal signals, teachers can help to surface and deal with emotional elements in every lesson, no matter what the subject area. Likewise they can take moments of personal crisis and turn them into lessons in emotional competence.

SEL Super Strategy: The Sharing Circle

To achieve its goals, *Social-Emotional Learning Activities for the Elementary Grades* incorporates a variety of proven instructional strategies. Activities include simulations, role plays, "experience sheets" for individual students to complete, and a host of small and large group experiments and discussions.

One of the most powerful and versatile of the instructional strategies used in this curriculum is the Sharing Circle. In each unit, six Sharing Circles are fully elaborated. These are followed by a list of additional Sharing Circle topics relevant to the unit topic. At first glance, the Sharing Circle — a small-group discussion process — is likely to appear deceptively simple. It is not. When used correctly, the Sharing Circle is unusually effective as a tool for developing self-awareness, the ability to understand and manage feelings, self-concept, personal responsibility, empathy, communication and group interaction skills.

The Sharing Circle is an ideal way to incorporate emotional learning in the classroom on a regular basis. First, the Sharing Circle provides safety, security, unconditional love and nurturing to each child. Second, Sharing Circle structure and procedures constitute a marked departure from traditional classroom teaching/learning approaches. Topics are stimulating in their ability to provoke self-inquiry. The ambiance is close yet respectful, over time causing intrapersonal defenses and interpersonal barriers to shrink and leading to new levels of group cohesiveness and creativity. Third, circle topics address real-life experiences and issues and the full range of emotions associated with them. And finally, the immediacy of the circle ensures that every child's contributions are heard and accepted on the spot. The attentiveness of other circle members along with their verbal and nonverbal emotional and cognitive reactions constitute a legitimate and powerful form of affirming feedback.

Please take the time to read the following sections before leading your first circle. Once you are familiar with the process, implement Sharing Circles regularly and as frequently as you can.

An Overview of the Sharing Circle

Decades of teaching the Sharing Circle process to educators world wide have demonstrated the power of the Sharing Circle in contributing to the development of SEL skills. To take full advantage of this process there are some things you need to know.

First, the topic elaboration provided under the heading, "Introduce the Topic," in each Sharing Circle is intended as a guide and does not have to be read verbatim. Once you have used Sharing Circles for a while and are feeling comfortable with the process, you will undoubtedly want to substitute your own words of introduction. We are merely providing you with ideas.

In your elaboration, try to use language and examples that are appropriate to the age, ability, and culture of your students. In our examples, we have attempted to be as general as possible; however, those examples may not be the most appropriate for your students.

Second, we strongly urge you to respect the integrity of the sharing and discussion phases of the circle. These two phases are procedurally and qualitatively different, yet of equal importance in promoting awareness, insight, and higher-level thinking in students. The longer you lead Sharing Circles, the more you will appreciate the instructional advantages of maintaining this unique relationship.

All Sharing Circle topics are intended to develop awareness and insight through voluntary sharing. The discussion questions allow students to understand what has been shared at deeper levels, to evaluate ideas that have been generated by the topic, and to apply specific concepts to other areas of learning.

In order for students to lead fulfilling, productive lives, to interact effectively with others, and to become adept at understanding and responding appropriately to the emotions of others, they first need to become aware of themselves and their own emotions. They need to know who they are, how they feel and function, and how they relate to others.

When used regularly, the *process* of the Sharing Circle coupled with its *content* (specific discussion topics) provides students with frequent opportunities to become more aware of their strengths, abilities, and positive qualities. In the Sharing Circle, students are listened to when they express their feelings and ideas, and they learn to listen to each other. The Sharing Circle format provides a framework in which genuine attention

and acceptance can be given and received on a consistent basis.

By sharing their experiences and feelings in a safe environment, students are able to see basic commonalties among human beings — and individual differences, too. This understanding contributes to the development of self-respect. On a foundation of self-respect, students grow to understand and respect others.

As an instructional tool, the purpose of the Sharing Circle is to promote growth and development in students of all ages. Targeted growth areas include communication, self-awareness, personal mastery, and interpersonal skills. As students follow the rules and relate to each other verbally during the Sharing Circle, they are practicing oral communication and learning to listen. Through insights developed in the course of pondering and discussing the various topics, students are offered the opportunity to grow in awareness and to feel more masterful — more in control of their feelings, thoughts, and behaviors. Through the positive experience of give and take, they learn more about effective modes of social interaction.

The Value of Listening

Many of us do not realize that merely listening to students talk can be immensely facilitating to their personal development. We do not need to diagnose, probe, or problem solve to help students focus attention on their own needs and use the information and insights in their own minds to arrive at their own conclusions. Because being listened to gives students confidence in their ability to positively affect their own lives, listening is certainly the facilitative method with the greatest long-term payoff.

When a student is dealing with a problem, or when her emotional state clearly indicates that something is bothering her, active listening is irreplaceable as a means of helping.

The Sharing Circle provides the opportunity for students to talk while others actively listen. By being given this opportunity, students gain important self-knowledge. Once they see that we do not intend to change them and that they may speak freely without threat of being "wrong," students find it easier to examine themselves and begin to see areas where they can make positive change in their lives. Just through the consistent process of sharing in a safe environment, students develop the ability to clarify their feelings and thoughts. They are encouraged to go deeper, find their own direction, and express and face strong feelings that may at other times be hidden obstacles to their growth. The important point is that students really can solve their own problems, develop self-awareness, and learn skills that will enable them to become responsible members of society if they are listened to effectively.

Awareness

Words are the only tool we have for systematically turning our attention and awareness to the feelings within us, and for describing and reflecting on our thoughts and behaviors. Feelings, after all, lead people to marry, to seek revenge, to launch war, to create great works of art, and to commit their lives to the service of others. They are vital and compelling.

For students to be able to manage their feelings, they must know what those feelings are. To know what they are, they must practice describing them in words. When a particular feeling is grasped in words several times, the mind soon begins to automatically recall ideas and concepts in association with the feeling and can start to provide ways of dealing with the feeling; e.g., "I'm feeling angry and I need to get away from this situation to calm down."

With practice, the mind becomes more and more adept at making these connections. When a recognized feeling comes up, the mind can sort through alternative responses to the feeling. As a student practices this response sequence in reaction to a variety of feelings, he will find words floating into consciousness that accurately identify what is going on emotionally and physically for him. This knowledge in turn develops the capacity to think before and during action. One mark of high emotional intelligence is the ability to recognize one's feelings and to take appropriate, responsible action. The ability to put words to feelings, to understand those words, to sort through an internal repertoire of responses and to choose appropriate, responsible behavior in reaction to a feeling indicates a high level of self-awareness and emotional intelligence.

By verbally exploring their own experiences in the Sharing Circle and listening to others do the same, all in an environment of safety, students are gently and gradually prompted to explore deeper within themselves and to grow and expand in their understanding of others. As this mutual sharing takes place, they learn that feelings, thoughts, and behaviors are real and experienced by everyone. They see others succeeding and failing in the same kinds of ways they succeed and fail. They also begin to see each person as unique and to realize that they are unique, too. Out of this understanding, students experience a growing concern for others. A sense of responsibility develops as the needs, problems, values, and preferences of others penetrate their awareness.

Personal Mastery

Personal mastery can be defined as self-confidence together with responsible competence. Self-confidence is believing in oneself as a capable human being. Responsible competence is the willingness to take responsibility for one's actions coupled with the ability to demonstrate fundamental human relations skills (competencies).

Through participation in Sharing Circles, students are encouraged to explore their successes and hear positive comments about their efforts. Many Sharing Circle topics heighten students' awareness of their own successes and those of others. Failure, or falling short, is a reality that is also examined. The focus, however, is not to remind students that they have failed; instead these topics enable students to see that falling short is common and universal and is experienced by all people when they strive to accomplish things.

Sharing Circle topics often address human relations competencies, such as the ability to include others, assume and share responsibility, offer help, behave assertively, solve problems, resolve conflicts, etc. Such topics elevate awareness in the human relations domain and encourage students to more effectively exercise these competencies and skills each day. The first step in a student's developing any competency is knowing that he or she is capable of demonstrating it. The Sharing Circle is particularly adept at helping students to recognize and acknowledge their own capabilities.

A particularly important element of personal mastery is personal responsibility. By focusing on their positive behaviors and accomplishments, the attention of students is directed toward the internal and external rewards that can be gained when they behave responsibly.

The Sharing Circle is a wonderful tool for teaching cooperation. As equitably as possible, the circle structure attempts to meet the needs of all participants. Everyone's feelings are accepted. Comparisons and judgments are not made. The circle is not another competitive arena, but is guided by a spirit of collaboration. When students practice fair, respectful interaction with one another, they benefit from the experience and are likely to employ these responsible behaviors in other life situations.

Interpersonal Skills

Relating effectively to others is a challenge we all face. People who are effective in their social interactions have the ability to understand others. They know how to interact flexibly, skillfully, and responsibly. At the same time, they recognize their own needs and maintain their own integrity. Socially effective people can process the nonverbal as well as verbal messages of others. They possess the very important awareness that all people have the power to affect one another. They are aware of not only how others affect them, but the effects their behaviors have on others.

The Sharing Circle process has been designed so that healthy, responsible behaviors are modeled by the teacher or counselor in his or her role as circle leader. The rules also require that the students relate positively and effectively to one another. The Sharing Circle brings out and affirms the positive qualities inherent in everyone and allows students to practice effective modes of communication. Because Sharing Circles provide a place where participants are listened to and their feelings accepted, students learn how to provide the same conditions to peers and adults outside the circle.

One of the great benefits of the Sharing Circle is that it does not merely teach young people about social interaction, it lets them interact! Every Sharing Circle is a real-life experience of social interaction where the students share, listen, explore, plan, dream, and problem solve together. As they interact, they learn about each other and they realize what it takes to relate effectively to others. Any given Sharing Circle may provide a dozen tiny flashes of positive interpersonal insight for an individual participant. Gradually, the reality of what constitutes effective behavior in relating to others is internalized.

Through this regular sharing of interpersonal experiences, the students learn that behavior can be positive or negative, and sometimes both at the same time. Consequences can be constructive, destructive, or both. Different people respond differently to the same event. They have different feelings and thoughts. The students begin to understand what will cause what to happen; they grasp the concept of cause and effect; they see themselves affecting others and being affected by others.

The ability to make accurate interpretations and responses in social interactions allows students to know where they stand with themselves and with others. They can tell what actions "fit" a situation. Sharing Circles are marvelous testing grounds where students can observe themselves and others in action, and can begin to see themselves as contributing to the good and bad feelings of others. With this understanding, students are helped to conclude that being responsible towards others feels good, and is the most valuable and personally rewarding form of interaction.

How to Conduct Sharing Circles

This section is a thorough guide for conducting Sharing Circles. It covers major points to keep in mind and answers questions which will arise as you begin using the program. Please remember that these guidelines are presented to assist you, not to restrict you. Follow them, and trust your own leadership style at the same time.

The Sharing Circle is a structured communication process that provides students a safe place for learning about life and developing important aspects of social-emotional learning.

First, we'll provide a brief overview of the process of leading a Sharing Circle and then we'll cover each step in more detail.

A Sharing Circle begins when a group of students and the adult leader sit down together in a circle so that each person is able to see the others easily. The leader of the Sharing Circle briefly greets and welcomes each individual, conveying a feeling of enthusiasm blended with seriousness.

During the first few Sharing Circles and while the children are still learning about the rules, the leader takes a few moments to review the Sharing Circle Rules. These rules inform the students of the positive behaviors required of them and guarantees the emotional safety and security, and equality of each member.

When everyone appears comfortable and after the students understand and agree to follow the rules, the leader announces the topic for the session. A brief elaboration of the topic follows in which the

leader provides examples and possibly mentions the topics relationship to prior topics or to other things the students are involved in. Then the leader re-states the topic and allows a little silence during which circle members may review and ponder their own related memories and mentally prepare their verbal response to the topic. (The topics and elaborations are provided in this curriculum.)

Next, the leader invites the circle participants to voluntarily share their responses to the topic, one at a time. No one is forced to share, but everyone is given an opportunity to share while all the other circle members listen attentively. The circle participants tell the group about themselves, their personal experiences, thoughts, feelings, hopes and dreams as they relate to the topic. Most of the circle time is devoted to this sharing phase because of its central importance.

During this time, the leader assumes a dual role—that of leader and participant. The leader makes sure that everyone who wishes to speak is given the opportunity while simultaneously enforcing the rules as necessary. The leader also takes a turn to speak if he or she wishes.

After everyone who wants to share has done so, the leader introduces the next phase of the Sharing Circle by asking several discussion questions. This phase represents a transition to the intellectual mode and allows participants to reflect on and express learnings gained from the sharing phase and encourages participants to combine cognitive abilities and emotional experiencing. It's in this phase that participants are able to crystallize learnings and to understand the relevance of the discussion to their daily lives. (Discussion questions for each topic are provided in this curriculum.)

When the students have finished discussing their responses to the questions and the session has reached a natural closure, the leader ends the session. The leader thanks the students for being part of the Sharing Circle and states that it is over.

What follows is a more detailed look at the process of leading a Sharing Circle.

Steps for Leading a Sharing Circle

1. Welcome Sharing Circle members
2. Review the Sharing Circle rules *
3. Introduce the topic
4. Sharing by circle members
5. Ask discussion questions
6. Close the circle

*optional after the first few sessions

---

1. Welcome Sharing Circle members

As you sit down with the students in a Sharing Circle group, remember that you are not teaching a lesson. You are facilitating a group of people. Establish a positive atmosphere. In a relaxed manner, address each student by name, using eye contact and conveying warmth. An attitude of seriousness blended with enthusiasm will let the students know that this Sharing Circle group is an important learning experience—an activity that can be interesting and meaningful.

2. Review the Sharing Circle rules

At the beginning of the first few Sharing Circles, and at appropriate intervals thereafter, go over the rules for the circle. They are:

Sharing Circle Rules

- Everyone gets a turn to share, including the leader.
- You can skip your turn if you wish.
- Listen to the person who is sharing.
- There are no interruptions, probing, put-downs, or gossip.
- Share the time equally.

From this point on, demonstrate to the students that you expect them to remember and abide by the ground rules. Convey that you think well of them and know they are fully capable of responsible behavior. Let them know that by coming to the Sharing Circle they are making a commitment to listen and show acceptance and respect for the other students and you. It is helpful to write the rules on chart paper and keep them on display for the benefit of each Sharing Circle session.

3. Introduce the topic

State the topic, and then in your own words, elaborate and provide examples as each Sharing Circle lesson in this book suggests. The introduction or elaboration of the topic is designed to get students focused and thinking about how they will respond to the topic. By providing more than just the mere statement of the topic, the elaboration gives students a few moments to expand their thinking and to make a personal connection to the topic at hand. Add clarifying statements of your own that will help the students understand the topic. Answer questions about the topic, and emphasize that there are no "right" responses. Finally, restate the topic, opening the session to responses (theirs and yours). Sometimes taking your turn first helps the students understand the aim of the topic. The introductions, as written in this book, are provided to give you some general ideas for opening the Sharing Circle. It's important that you adjust and modify the introduction and elaboration to suit the ages, abilities, levels, cultural/ethnic backgrounds and interests of your students.

4. Sharing by circle members

The most important point to remember is this: The purpose of these Sharing Circles is to give students an opportunity to express themselves and be accepted for the experiences, thoughts, and feelings they share. Avoid taking the action away from the students. They are the stars!

5. Ask discussion questions

Responding to discussion questions is the cognitive portion of the process. During this phase, the leader asks thought-provoking questions to stimulate free discussion and higher-level thinking. Each Sharing Circle lesson in this book concludes with several discussion questions. At times, you may want to formulate questions that are more appropriate to the level of understanding in your students—or to what was actually shared in the circle. If you wish to make connections between the topic and your content area, ask questions that will accomplish that objective and allow the answering of the discussion questions to extend longer. We have left a space on each page for you

to note significant other questions that you create and find effective.

6. Close the circle

The ideal time to end a Sharing Circle is when the discussion question phase reaches natural closure. Sincerely thank everyone for being part of the circle. Don't thank specific students for speaking, as doing so might convey the impression that speaking is more appreciated than mere listening. Then close the group by saying, "This Sharing Circle is over," or "OK, that ends our circle."

More about Sharing Circle Steps and Rules

The next few paragraphs offer further clarification concerning leadership of Sharing Circles.

Who gets to talk? Everyone. The importance of acceptance cannot be overly stressed. In one way or another practically every ground rule says one thing: accept one another. When you model acceptance of students, they will learn how to be accepting. Each individual in the group is important and deserves a turn to speak if he or she wishes to take it. Equal opportunity to become involved should be given to everyone in the Sharing Circle.

Members should be reinforced equally for their contributions. There are many reasons why a leader may become more enthused over what one student shares than another. The response may be more on target, reflect more depth, be more entertaining, be philosophically more in keeping with one's own point of view, and so on. However, students need to be given equal recognition for their contributions, even if the contribution is to listen silently throughout the session.

In most of the Sharing Circles, plan to take a turn and address the topic, too. Students usually appreciate it very much and learn a great deal when their teachers, counselors, and other adults are willing to tell about their own experiences, thoughts, and feelings. In this way you let your students know that you acknowledge your own humanness.

Does everyone have to take a turn? No. Students may choose to skip their turns. If the circle becomes a pressure situation in which the members are coerced in any way to speak, it will become an unsafe place where participants are not comfortable. Meaningful discussion is unlikely in such an atmosphere. By allowing students to make this choice, you are showing them that you accept their right to remain silent if that is what they choose to do.

As you begin the circle, it's important to remember that it's not a problem if one or more students decline to speak. If you are imperturbable and accepting when this happens, you let them know you are offering them an opportunity to experience something you think is valuable, or at least worth a try, and not attempting to force-feed them. You as a leader should not feel compelled to share a personal experience in every session, either. However, if you decline to speak in most of the sessions, this may have an inhibiting effect on the students' willingness to share.

Some leaders ask the participants to raise their hands when they wish to speak, while others simply allow free verbal sharing without soliciting the leader's permission first. Choose the procedure that works best for you, but do not call on anyone unless you can see signs of readiness. And do not merely go around the circle.

Some leaders have reported that their first group fell flat—that no one, or just one or two students, had anything to say. But they continued to have groups, and at a certain point everything changed. Thereafter, the students had a great deal to say that these leaders considered worth waiting for. It appears that in these cases the leaders' acceptance of the right to skip turns was a key factor. In time most students will contribute verbally when they have something they want to say, and when they are assured there is no pressure to do so.

Sometimes a silence occurs during a session. Don't feel you have to jump in every time someone stops talking. During silences students have an opportunity to think about what they would like to share or to contemplate an important idea they've heard. A general rule of thumb is to allow silence to the point that you observe group discomfort. At that point move on. Do not switch to another topic. To do so implies you will not be satisfied until the students speak. If you change to another topic, you are telling them you didn't really mean it when you said they didn't have to take a turn if they didn't want to.

If you are bothered about students who attend a number of sessions and still do not share verbally, reevaluate what you consider to be involvement. Participation does not necessarily mean talking. Students who do not speak are listening and learning.

How can I encourage effective listening? The Sharing Circle is a time (and place) for students and leaders to strengthen the habit of listening by doing it over and over again. No one was born knowing how to listen effectively to others. It is a skill like any other that gets better as it is practiced. In the immediacy of the Sharing Circle the members become keenly aware of the necessity to listen, and most students respond by expecting it of one another.

In these Sharing Circles, listening is defined as the respectful focusing of attention on individual speakers. It includes eye contact with the speaker and open body posture. It eschews interruptions of any kind. When you lead a circle, listen and encourage listening in the students by (l) focusing your attention on the person who is speaking, (2) being receptive to what the speaker is saying (not mentally planning your next remark), and (3) recognizing the speaker when she finishes speaking, either verbally ("Thanks, Shirley") or nonverbally (a nod and a smile).

To encourage effective listening in the students, reinforce them by letting them know you have noticed they were listening to each other and you appreciate it.

How can I ensure the students get equal time?
When group members share the time equally, they demonstrate their acceptance of the notion that everyone's contribution is of equal importance. It is not uncommon to have at least one dominator in a group. This person is usually totally unaware that by continuing to talk he or she is taking time from others who are less assertive. An important social skill is knowing how you affect others in a group and when dominating a group is inappropriate behavior.

Be very clear with the students about the purpose of this ground rule. Tell them at the outset how much time there is. When it is your turn, always limit your own contribution. If someone goes on and on, do intervene (dominators need to know what they are doing), but do so as gently and respectfully as you can.

What are some examples of put-downs?
Put-downs convey the message, "You are not okay as you are." Some put-downs are deliberate, but many are made unknowingly. Both kinds are undesirable in a Sharing Circle because they destroy the atmosphere of acceptance and disrupt the flow of sharing and discussion. Typical put-downs include:

- over questioning.
- statements that have the effect of teaching or preaching
- advice giving
- one-upsmanship
- criticism, disapproval, or objections
- sarcasm
- statements or questions of disbelief

How can I deal with put-downs?
There are two major ways for dealing with put-downs: preventing them from occurring and intervening when they do.

Going over the rules with the students at the beginning of each Sharing Circle, particularly in the earliest sessions, is a helpful preventive technique. Another is to reinforce the students when they adhere to the rule. Be sure to use non patronizing, non evaluative language.

Unacceptable behavior should be stopped the moment it is recognized by the leader. When you become aware that a put-down is occurring, do whatever you ordinarily do to stop destructive behavior. If one student gives another an unasked-for bit of advice, say for example, "Jane, please give Alicia a chance to tell her story." To a student who interrupts say, "Ed, it's Sally's turn." In most cases the fewer words, the better—students automatically tune out messages delivered as lectures.

Sometimes students disrupt the group by starting a private conversation with the person next to them. Touch the offender on the arm or shoulder while continuing to give eye contact to the student who is speaking. If you can't reach the offender, simply remind him or her of the rule about listening.

If students persist in putting others down or disrupt the circle, ask to see them at another time and hold a brief one-to-one conference, urging them to follow the rules. Suggest that they reconsider their membership in the group. Make it clear that if they don't intend to honor the rules, they are not to come to the group.

How can I keep students from gossiping?
Periodically remind students that using names and sharing embarrassing information in a Sharing Circle is not acceptable. Urge the students to relate personally to one another, but not to tell intimate details of their lives.

What should the leader do during the discussion question phase? Conduct this part of the process as an open forum, giving students the opportunity to discuss a variety of ideas and accept those that make sense to them. Don't impose your opinions on the students, or allow the students to impose theirs on one another. Ask open-ended questions, encourage higher-level thinking, contribute your own ideas when appropriate, and act as a facilitator.

In Conclusion: The Two Most Important Things to Remember

No matter what happens in a Sharing Circle session, the following two elements are the most critcal:

1. Everyone gets a turn.
2. Everyone who takes a turn gets listened to with respect.

What does it mean to get a turn? Imagine a pie divided into as many pieces as there are people in the group. Telling the students that everyone gets a turn, whether they want to take it or not, is like telling them that each one gets a piece of the pie. Some students may not want their piece right away, but they know it's there to take when they do want it. As the teacher or counselor, you must protect this shared ownership. Getting a turn not only represents a chance to talk, it is an assurance that every member of the group has a "space" that no one else will violate.

When students take their turn, they will be listened to. There will be no attempt by anyone to manipulate what a student is offering. That is, the student will not be probed, interrupted, interpreted, analyzed, put-down, joked-at, advised, preached to, and so on. To "listen to" is to respectfully focus attention on the speaker and to let the speaker know that you have heard what he or she has said.

In the final analysis, the only way that a Sharing Circle can be evaluated is against these two criteria. Thus, if only two students choose to speak, but are listened to—even if they don't say very "deep" or "meaningful" things—the discussion group can be considered a success.

Bibliography and Resources

Durlak, J. A., Domitrovich, C. E., Weissberg, R. P., and Gullotta, T. P. (Eds.). *Handbook of Social and Emotional Learning: Research and Practice.* Guilford Press, 2015

Elias, M. J. and Arnold, H. *The Educators Guide to Emotional Intelligence and Academic Achievement: Social-Emotional Learning in the Classroom.* Corwin Press, 2006

Gardner, Howard. *Frames of Mind: Theory of Multiple Intelligence.* Fontana Press, 1993.

Goleman, Daniel. *Tenth Anniversary Edition, Emotional Intelligence: Why It Can Matter More than IQ.* Random House, 2006

Goleman, Daniel. *Social Intelligence: The New Science of Human Relationships.* Random House, 2006

Lantieri, Linda. *Building Emotional Intelligence: Techniques to Cultivate Inner Strength in Children.* Soundstrue, 2008

Web Sites

CASEL.org

> Collaborative for Academic, Social, and Emotional Learning

Edutopia.org

> George Lucas Educational Foundation

Steps for Leading a Sharing Circle

1. Welcome Sharing Circle members

2. Review the Sharing Circle rules *

3. Introduce the topic

4. Sharing by circle members

5. Ask discussion questions

6. Close the circle

   *optional after the first few sessions

Sharing Circle
Rules

- Everyone gets a turn to share, including the leader.

- You can skip your turn if you wish.

- Listen to the person who is sharing.

- There are no interruptions, probing, put-downs, or gossip.

- Share the time equally.

Self-Awareness

Who Am I?
Experience Sheet and Discussion

Objectives: | The students will:
—identify individual interests, abilities, strengths, and weaknesses.
—define individual differences as contributing to personal uniqueness.

Materials: | one copy of the experience sheet, "This is Me!," for each student

Procedure: | Pass out a copy of the experience sheet to each student. Read the directions to them. Explain that they will have about 10 minutes to complete the experience sheet, and will then be asked to join you for a discussion. Tell the students that it will be interesting to find out what they think about themselves. Distribute the copies of the experience sheet and, if possible, circulate as the students complete them. Offer assistance as needed. Lead a follow-up discussion.

Discussion Questions: | — Which words did you choose to describe yourself?
— What are some of the things that you enjoy doing?
— What are some of the things that you do well?
— Do our experience sheets look different from one another? Why is that?
— Why is it important to get to know ourselves and each other in ways like this?

This Is Me!
Experience Sheet

1. Draw a red circle around words that describe you.
2. Draw a blue circle around words that name things you enjoy doing.
3. Draw a green circle around words that name things you do well.
   It's okay to draw more than one circle around the same word.

drawing	helping at home	cooking
running	short	collecting things
using a computer	reading	carrots
brown hair	blonde bair	tall
chocolate milk	acting	flowers
dancing	listening to music	pony tail
doing puzzles	brown skin	tennis shoes
talking with friends	wear glasses	yogurt
green eyes	writing	kittens
friendly	freckles	going barefoot
boy	hula hoops	curly hair
arithmetic	computer games	_____
ice cream	painting	_____
science	helping at school	_____
swimming	red hair	_____
playing a musical instrument	having a pet	_____
girl	gardening	_____

The Write Stuff
A Vocabulary for Feelings

Objectives: The students will:
—acquaint themselves with a variety of feelings words and their meanings.
—demonstrate an understanding of new feeling words.

Materials: one copy of the experience sheet, "So Many Ways to Feel" for each student; writing paper and pencils

Procedure: Begin by asking the students to help you brainstorm words that describe feelings. Cover the board with these words.

Ask volunteers to choose a word from the list and describe a real or hypothetical situation that causes them to feel this way. For example, a student who chooses the word "exasperated," might explain that having to pick up a younger sister's dirty clothes makes her feel exasperated.

After many students have shared their situations using the words on the board, distribute the experience sheets. Give the students several minutes to look over the words, and then ask volunteers to name those that are unfamiliar. Discuss the meaning of the words with the entire group.

Explain to the students that they are going to have an opportunity to practice using words from the list that they have not previously used. Ask the students to choose 5 words from the list, and to use these words in five sentences — one sentence demonstrating a correct meaning and context for each word. Tell the students that they may use any of the following suggestions in creating their sentences:

1. Use a sentence pattern: "I feel/felt (new feeling word) when (something happens/happened)."
2. If possible, change a word to an adverb by adding *ly* and use it to describe an action: "I jealously watched as my opponent received the gold medal in the 100 yard dash."
3. Use the word in a sentence that tells why someone feels/felt that way: "The miserable woman trudged another five miles through the snow looking for a service station where she could buy gas for her stalled car."

When the students have completed their sentences, ask them to form dyads and to read their sentences to their partner. Invite the partners to give each other feedback — for example, which sentence they liked best and why. Then gather the group together and invite volunteers to share a sentence. Finish with a general discussion.

Discussion Questions:

— Why is it beneficial to know lots of feeling words?
— What good does it do to have so many words to describe similar feelings?
— Which words on the list have you felt before, without knowing their names? Which words have you known before, without ever experiencing the feeling?

So Many Ways to Feel
Experience Sheet

abandoned
accepted
adamant
adequate
affectionate
afraid
agonized
alarmed
alienated
ambivalent
annoyed
anxious
apathetic
appreciated
astounded
attractive
awed
awkward

bad
beaten
beautiful
betrayed
bewildered
bitter
blissful
bold
bored
brave
burdened

comfortable
concerned
confident
connected
cop-out, like a
cowardly
creative
curious
cut off from others

deceitful
defeated
dejected
delighted
dependent

depressed
deprived
desperate
destructive
determined
different
diffident
diminished
disappointed
discontented
distracted
distraught
disturbed
divided
dominated
dubious

eager
ecstatic
elated
electrified
embarrassed
empty
enchanted
energetic
envious
evasive
exasperated
excited
exhausted
exhilarated

fawning
fearful
flustered
foolish
frantic
free
friendless
friendly
frightened
frustrated
full

glad
good

grateful
gratified
greedy
grieving
groovy
guilty
gullible
gutles

happy
hateful
helpful
helpless
high
homesick
honored
hopeful
hopeless
horrible
hostile
hurt
hysterical

ignored
immobilized
impatient
imposed upon
impressed
inadequate
incompetent
in control
indecisive
independent
infatuated
inferior
infuriated
inhibited
insecure
insincere
inspired
intimidated
involved
isolated
jealous
joyous

judgmental
jumpy

lazy
left out
lonely
loser, like a
lovable
loving
low
loyal

manipulated
miserable
misunderstood

needy
nervous
nice

odd
opposed
optimistic
outraged
overlooked
overwhelmed

panicked
paranoid
peaceful
persecuted
petrified
pleasant
pleased
possessive
preoccupied
pressured

quarrelsome
quiet

refreshed
rejected
relaxed
relieved
remorseful
repulsive

restless
restrained

sad
satisfied
scared
screwed up
settled
shallow
shocked
shy
silly
sluggish
sorry
spiritual
strained
stunned
stupid
sure

tempted
tense
threatened
thwarted
tired
torn
touched
touchy
trapped
troubled

unappreciated
uncertain
uneasy
unsettled
uptight
used

violent
vivacious
vulnerable

wishy-washy
wonderful
worried

It's In the Bag
Speaking/Collecting Activity

Objectives:	The students will: —select and share items that have special meaning to them. —identify and describe aspects of themselves and their lives.
Materials:	'Me" bags (one per child) containing things that represent the children's interests. (See procedure)
Procedure:	One class session before this activity, ask the students to gather pictures, treasures, and memorabilia, place them in a brown paper bag, and bring the bag to the next class. Show them an example, by displaying a bag of your own memorabilia. Have the students form a circle with their bags in front of them. Ask for volunteers, or draw names, to determine the order of sharing. In your own words, explain the activity: *Pick items from your bag, show them, and tell the group what each is and why it is important to you. Tell us if the item is something you like or dislike, and how you came to have this thing. For example, you might explain that you brought a teddy bear that you have had since you were little. Or you might show a picture of a ballerina because you want to take dance lessons and would like to be a performer someday, or a picture of a baseball player because that is a game you like to play.* Some of the students may need a little prompting from you during the sharing process. When a student is shy or reluctant, ask questions like, "Was that a gift?" or "Would you like to tell us why that is important to you?" After the sharing, have the students return to their regular seating. Lead a brief follow-up discussion.
Discussion Questions:	— How did you feel when you were sharing your treasures and memorabilia? — Did anyone include items that represent things they do not enjoy or that give them bad feelings? Why? — When you think about your special item how does it make you feel? — What do you think your bag of treasures says about you? What message does it convey?

Winning Qualities
Experience Sheet and Discussion

Objectives: The children will:
—describe positive characteristics in themselves.
—demonstrate a positive attitude toward themselves.
—identify interests, abilities, and strengths as components of personal uniqueness.

Materials: pencils for writing; one copy of the experience sheet, "Winning Qualities: Write a Sentence About Yourself!" for each student.

Procedure: Distribute the experience sheets. Read aloud the directions at the top of the experience sheet. Tell the students that they will have 10 minutes to complete the sheet. Explain that they will then have the opportunity to share their sentences with two classmates.

Have the students begin filling out the experience sheet. Circulate and lend assistance, as needed.

Have the students share their completed experience sheets in groups of three. Group students who are already seated near one another and who get along well. Tell the students to take turns reading their sentences.

When the small group discussions are concluded, gather all the groups together and lead a culminating discussion.

Discussion Questions:
— How does it feel to talk about yourself in this way to others?
— Why is it good to say nice things about ourselves?
— Why do you think it feels strange to complement yourself?

Winning Qualities: Write a Sentence about Yourself!

Experience Sheet

Here are three lists of words. On each list, check the words that describe you best, or write a word or two of your own on each list.

1. Adjective (pick 2)	**2. Noun (pick 1)**	**3. Action verb (pick 2)**
friendly	student	enjoys other people
polite	boy	learns quickly
honest	girl	works hard
dependable	person	is good at _____
cooperative	friend	achieves in school
creative		is great at _____
enthusiastic	_____	gets along well with others
smart		is fun to be with
	_____	has good ideas
_____		
_____		

Now, write a sentence that describes you. Write the words you checked in the blanks, as shown:

I am a _____ and _____ _____
      (from list 1)   (from list 1)   (from list 2)

who _____ and
                      (from list 3)

_____ .
             (from list 3)

Images of Me
Art Activity

Objectives: The students will:
— graphically represent three different images of themselves.
— view and talk about the significance of each image and the feelings it engenders.

Materials: large shapes (circle, triangle, rectangle, etc.) cut from colored construction paper (at least three shapes per student); large sheets of white poster board or construction paper; colored markers, crayons, scissors, and glue

Procedure: Introduce the concept of self-image. Explain that an image is a picture of something. It can be a photograph or drawing, and it can also be the image we see in our mind when we *think about* the real thing. Self-image is how we mentally see ourselves.

In your own words, explain further: *Each of us may have several different self-images. You may have one image when you think of yourself at home with your family, and a very different one when you think of yourself playing baseball with your friends. Today, I want you to think of three of the best images you have of yourself and draw them. Then, use those three drawings to design a poster all about you.*

Give each student three different construction-paper shapes, and ask a couple of students to distribute scissors, markers/crayons, glue, and poster board. While the students are getting set up, write the following list on the board:

My Family and Me
Me and My Friends
A Favorite Place
A Favorite Possession
My Pet and Me
A Favorite Day of the Year
A Dream Vacation
A Favorite Game or Sport
My Best School Subject
Something I'm Proud Of

Read through the list with the students, and explain: *Choose any topic from the list, and write the topic at the top of one of your shapes. Draw a picture on that shape, showing the image you have of yourself when you think of that topic. Then, choose two more topics and illustrate those on your remaining two shapes. When you have illustrated all three shapes, move the shapes around on a sheet of poster board until you come up with a design that you like. Finally, glue the shapes in place. Title your poster, "Images of (your name)."*

Circulate during the work phase of the activity, and engage the students in brief conversations about their pictures. When the posters are finished, one at a time have the students hold up their poster and briefly describe what is happening in each of the three pictures. Facilitate a culminating discussion about the importance of having positive self-images. Finally, display the posters around the room.

Discussion Questions:

— When you imagine yourself in a positive picture, how do you feel?
— When your image of yourself is poor, how do you feel?
— Where do we get the images we have of ourselves?
— Why is it important to see ourselves in positive ways?

Variations:

Provide several patterns, and have the students cut out their own shapes, or have them trace around the patterns to make the images directly on the poster board.

Strength Bombardment
A Game of Appreciation

Objectives: The students will:
—become more aware of their own strengths and those of others.
—hear numerous positive statements about themselves.
—practice giving positive feedback.

Materials: a small pad of self-sticking labels; one pencil and one large sheet of plain paper per student; chart paper and markers or whiteboard

Procedure: Tell the students that today you are going to focus on strengths. Ask: *Do you know what a strength is?*

Discuss the concept briefly, explaining that all people have strengths - good qualities, talents, and skills that others like and that make them successful. Point out that there are many words which name strengths, and ask the students to help you list some of them. On the board or chart paper, develop a list that includes such things as:

nice	funny
handsome	good sport
generous	honest
kind	plays the piano well
runs fast	writes great stories
smart	good in Math
friendly	loyal
pretty hair	respectful

Distribute the labels and pencils. Have the students label one sticker for each person in the class, writing the person's initials. You should participate in this, too.

Instruct the students to go back through their stickers and write a positive statement on each one. Tell them to think about the person, look at the list of strengths on the board/chart, and describe a quality or ability that they like in that person. Allow plenty of time for this phase of the activity.

Give each student a plain piece of paper. Tell the students to write their name at the top. Then, gather the class in a single large circle and explain the strength bombardment exercise.

In your own words, say: *One person at a time passes his or her sheet of paper around the circle. When the sheet comes to you, find the label you have made for that person and stick it on the sheet. Then look at the person, say his or her name, and describe the strength. You might say, "Ted, the strength I see in you is your humor." When it's your turn to receive strength statements, just listen and accept what people tell you. You may say "thank you," but that's all.*

Proceed with the strength bombardment. Afterwards, lead a brief summary discussion. Suggest that the students take their strength papers home, display them on a wall or bulletin board, and look at them often.

Discussion Questions:

— How did you feel when you were receiving strength statements?
— How did you feel when you were giving strength statements'?
— Why is it important to recognize our own strengths and those of others?

Act Out a Feeling!
Dramatization and Discussion

Objectives: The students will:
—identify feelings based on verbal and nonverbal cues.
—develop a working vocabulary for feeling words.
—state that feelings are natural and normal.
—describe the relationship between events and emotional reactions.

Materials: at least 12 strips of plain paper; one black fine-tip marking pen; one empty can (coffee can size is perfect)

Procedure: Tell the students that you have observed them displaying a lot of different feelings today, just as they do every day. Then describe a specific incident in which you were able to discern a person's feelings clearly. For example, describe how one person was hurt by the criticism or name-calling of another person. (Don't identify the individuals involved.) Ask the children if they noticed other incidents involving feelings, both positive and negative. Without naming names, discuss the various emotions demonstrated by people they (and you) observed.

As the students name feelings, write each feeling word down on a paper strip and put it in the can. After you have deposited a number of strips in the can, ask, "How can you tell by looking at a person how he or she feels?" After several responses, announce that the students are going to have an opportunity to act out the feelings they've been discussing.

Ask volunteers to come to the front of the room, draw a strip of paper from the can, and act out the feeling written on the paper. Emphasize that the students may express the feeling in any way they wish, using both body and face, but without naming the feeling. Explain that the rest of the class will try to guess what the feeling is. Give all volunteers an opportunity to participate.

Discussion Questions: Between dramatizations, facilitate discussion. Each time a new feeling is dramatized, ask the class these questions:
— What might cause a person to feel this way?
— Can you remember a time when you had this feeling? In just a few words, tell us what happened.

After each of the emotions has been dramatized several times, conclude the activity with these questions:
— What did you learn about feelings today?
— Does everyone have the feelings we acted out? How do you know?
— When you feel one of these feelings, or some other feeling, is it okay?
— What do you feel inside when you empathize with another person's feelings?
— When you feel angry or jealous, is it okay to do something that hurts another person? What can you do instead?

Who I Am on the Inside and Outside

Art Activity

Objectives: The students will:
—identify their own positive inner and outer qualities
—creatively symbolize their positive qualities in art.

Materials: shoe boxes or other containers on which pictures can be glued or drawn on both the outside and inside, magazines, colored paper, yarn, scraps of cloth, crayons or magic markers, scissors, and white glue

Directions: Place the materials on large tables or at other locations where the students will be working. Give each student a container. The students will glue an assortment of pictures from magazines, pieces of material, yarn, colored paper, and/or their own designs to the outside and inside of their containers.

Explain: *We will each decorate a container on the outside and inside to show our positive outer and inner qualities. On the outside, glue pictures, designs, and colored cloth that represent positive personal qualities that you would like to show others. Decorate the inside of the container to show some of the good inner feelings you have about yourself.*

As the students work, decorate a container yourself. Suggest that the students use pictures of kids having fun, beautiful colors or designs, and fabrics that seem to represent particular feelings or qualities. Let them be as creative as they wish, as long as their efforts are positive.

During the activity, talk to the students about positive qualities and feelings and the kinds of pictures and designs that can be used to represent them. Ask the students to talk about their choices, acknowledging them with appreciation.

When the students have completed their boxes allow them to show their decorated containers and talk about their inner and outer qualities.

Conclude the activity by asking these and other discussion questions.

Discussion Questions:

— Why is it important to understand both our inner feelings and outer projections of ourselves?
— In what ways is how you fell about yourself different from how others see you?
— What did you learn about yourself from this activity?

One of My Favorite Possessions
A Sharing Circle

Objectives:

The students will:
—identify and describe a valued possession.
—explain the nature and source of their feelings about the item.

Introduce the Topic:

All of us have possessions that we prize and value highly. We enjoy using them or perhaps we get pleasure from just looking at them. Today, we'll each have an opportunity to talk about something that is very special to us. Our topic is, "One of My Favorite Possessions."

You probably own several things that are special to you. You may have had some of these possessions since you were very young, and you have probably acquired others more recently. Tell us about one special thing you own, and describe what makes that item important to you. Someone you care for very much may have given it to you, or you may have done extra chores to earn enough money to buy it. The item could be something that's fun to wear, or play with, or work with. Or it might be an item that simply looks nice in your room. Think about it for a moment. The topic is, "One of My Favorite Possessions."

Discussion Questions:

— What is it that makes certain things special to us?
— Do you think it's important for people to have favorite possessions? Why or Why not?
— What did you learn about yourself or another person during this circle?

Something I Really Like To Do
A Sharing Circle

Objectives: The students will:
—describe a preferred activity.
—explain the feelings associated from a preferred activity.
—trace some of the sources of their likes, dislikes, and personal preferences.

Introduce the topic: *Our topic for today is "Something I Really Like To Do." There are probably many things that you like to do. However, today I'd like you to pick just one activity that you truly enjoy and tell us about it. Perhaps drawing pictures is a favorite activity of yours, or writing stories, or playing computer games. Maybe you enjoy swimming, dancing, or building models. Take a moment to think about it. When you're ready to share, raise your hand and tell us about "Something I Really Like To Do."*

Discussion Questions:
— What were the different activities mentioned in the circle?
— What determines whether you enjoy an activity or not?
— Why do people like to do different things?
— Where or how do we acquire our likes and dislikes?

Something I Did (or Made) That I'm Proud Of
A Sharing Circle

Objectives:

The students will:
—acknowledge themselves for things they've accomplished.
—describe feelings and bodily sensations associated with being proud.

Introduce the Topic:

Our topic for this session is, "Something I Did (or Made) That I'm Proud Of." Think of something that you accomplished that you feel very good about. It can be something you did, like an assignment, chore, sports activity, or special event. Or it can be something you made, like a drawing, a model, a photograph, or a scrapbook.

Maybe you helped solve a problem for a friend or family member. Or perhaps you made great party invitations, or played with a younger brother or sister so your mom could do something she needed to do. Maybe you baked a batch of cookies without burning a single one. Or maybe you learned how to play your favorite song on the piano without making any mistakes. Whatever it was, you feel proud that you were able to do it. Take a moment or two to think of something. The topic is, "Something I Did (or Made) That I'm Proud Of."

Discussion Questions:

— What kinds of things were we proud of?
— What difference is there between being pleased and being proud?
— What feelings and sensations do you have inside when you are proud?

Something I Like About Myself
A Sharing Circle

Objectives:

The students will:
—demonstrate a positive attitude about themselves.
—describe positive characteristics about themselves.

Introduce the Topic:

Today we are going to talk about something everybody loves to talk about. We will talk about ourselves — to say some very good and true things about ourselves. The topic is, "Something I Like About Myself."

Think about yourself for a few moments. You have so many good qualities that it may be hard to decide which one to talk about. Maybe you're glad to be yourself because you learn things so easily. Or maybe you are good at playing and having fun with your friends. Perhaps you like something about your body, like your curly hair or your freckles. Maybe you're proud of your ability to play games and sports well. Let's think about it for a moment. When you are ready to share, raise your hand. The topic is, "Something I Like About Myself."

Discussion Questions:

— Why is it okay for us to say what we like about ourselves in the Sharing Circle?
— Why is it good for us to take pride in ourselves?
— How do other people let you know that they are proud of you?

A Time I Felt Happy
A Sharing Circle

Objectives: The students will:
— describe situations in which they felt happy.
— verbalize positive feelings.

Introduce the topic: In your own words, tell the students: *Sometimes we feel happy and sometimes we don't—we feel unhappy. Today we are going to talk about happy feelings in our Sharing Circle. The topic is, "A Time I Felt Happy."*

Can you remember a time when you felt happy? Maybe something very nice happened and you felt good about it. Or perhaps someone did something for you that you really liked. Let's close our eyes and see if we can remember a time like that, okay? Think about it and when you look up at me, I'll know that you are ready to talk and listen. I'll say the topic again. It is, "A Time I Felt Happy."

Discussion Questions:
— What kinds of things caused us to feel happy?
— Why is it important to tell one another about times we felt happy?
— How do you feel when you remember times you felt happy?

A Time I Felt Unhappy
A Sharing Circle

Objectives: The students will:
— describe times when they experienced negative feelings.
— state that it is normal to feel unhappy at times.

Introduce the topic: In your own words, tell the students: *Our topic for today is, "A Time I Felt Unhappy." Everybody feels happy at times and everybody feels unhappy at other times. It's more fun for most people to tell about happy feelings, but sometimes it does us good to talk about unhappy feelings as well. Can you remember a time when you felt unhappy? Maybe you had an accident and got hurt, or perhaps you wanted something and you didn't get it so you were disappointed. If you would like to take a turn, tell us what made you unhappy and describe what the feeling was like for you, okay? Let's think about it for a moment. Then, when you are ready to share, raise your hand. The topic is, "A Time I Felt Unhappy."*

Discussion Questions: — What kinds of things caused us to feel unhappy?
— Why is it good for us to tell one another about times we felt unhappy?
— Why can't we be happy all the time?

Additional Sharing Circle Topics

A Person I Admire

A Secret Wish I Have

Something I Like to Do Alone

The Craziest Dream I Ever Had

One Way I Wish I Could Be Different

An Important Event in My Life

Something I Want to Keep

Something I Like to Do with Others

When I Felt Comfortable Just Being Me

Something I Need Help With

My Favorite Place

My Idea of a Perfect Saturday Afternoon

Something About My Culture That I Appreciate

The Funniest Thing That Ever Happened to Me

My Favorite Vacation

Something I Like to Do With My Family

My Favorite Daydream

One of the Best Things That Ever Happened to Me

Something About Me That You Wouldn't Know Unless I Told You

A Friend of Mine Who Is Different From Me

Something I Really Like to Do at School

If I Had One Wish It Would Be

One Way I Wish I Could Be Different

One Thing I Am Sure I Can Do Well

Something I Want

A Special Occasion or Holiday Related to My Culture

A Person I'd Like to Be Like

Self-Management

Positive Communication
Discussion and Experience Sheet

Objectives: | The students will:
— state that feelings can be communicated either positively or negatively.
— describe appropriate ways of expressing feelings.
— explain how one's actions affect the feelings of others.

Materials: | one copy of the experience sheet, "Communicating My Feelings," for each student

Procedure: | Write the heading, "Angry," on the board, and ask, "Who can tell me one way that you express yourself when you are angry?" Elicit several responses and, as succinctly as possible, record those responses in a column under the heading. Then ask, "Are these the best possible ways to respond when you're angry?"

Ask the students to brainstorm positive ways of handling anger. Accept all responses, but remind the students to keep their suggestions <u>positive</u>. Write these responses in a second column. When the second column is full, ask the following questions to facilitate discussion.

Discussion Questions: | — How do you feel when you behave in the ways we listed in the first column?
— Do these behaviors help you deal with your anger? Why or why not?
— How do you think people around you feel when you express yourself in these ways?
— How do you feel when you behave in the ways we listed in the second column?
— Do these methods help you deal with your anger? Why or why not?
— How do you think the people around you feel when you express yourself in these ways?

Pass out the experience sheet, "Communicating My Feelings," and go over the directions with the students. When the students have completed the experience sheet, ask volunteers to share their ideas concerning appropriate ways to express each feeling.

Communicating My Feelings
Experience Sheet

Everyone has feelings; they are a natural part of being human. We all share the same feelings, but we express those feelings in different ways. It is important for us to learn how to communicate our feelings appropriately.

Look at the feelings listed below. Describe in writing the things you do and say to express each feeling. Then see if you can think of a better way to express yourself, and write that down, too.

When I am angry, I usually express myself by: _____

_____

A better way to express my anger would be to: _____

_____

When I am sad, I usually express myself by: _____

_____

A better way to express my sadness would be to: _____

_____

When I am happy, I usually express myself by: _____

_____

A better way to express my happiness would be to: _____

_____

When I am discouraged, I usually express myself by: _____

_____

A better way to express my discouragement would be to: _____

_____

When I am scared, I usually express myself by: _____

_____

A better way to express my fear would be to: _____

_____

When I want attention I usually express myself by: _____

_____

A better way to receive attention would be to: _____

_____

No More Put Downs
Survey, Sharing and Discussion

Objectives: The students will:
—become aware of a common communication habit that is often hurtful to others and can damage relationships.
—understand reasons that people put down others.
—empathize with the receiver of put-down statements.

Materials: whiteboard

Procedure: Tell the class that you want to focus on a way of talking that is very common at school. Explain that talking this way often starts out as a form of joking around, or teasing, and then turns into a habit. Unfortunately, this habit of communication can be hurtful to others and serves no real purpose. Ask the students to guess what you are talking about. Give them a few moments and if no one guesses correctly, write "put downs" or "putting others down" on the board.

Ask the students to help you make a list of all the statements they remember hearing people say that put others down. As the students give you the words, write them on the board, enclosing each phrase in quotation marks.

Talk about the nature of put-downs. Ask the students:

— Why do people put each other down?
— Are some put downs worse than others?
— How can a person tell the difference between a put down that is meant as a joke and a put down that is intentionally hurtful?

Give the students the following assignment: *For the next 24 hours, carry a pencil and a piece of paper with you and write down every put-down statement you hear. Write down put downs that are directed at you, and put downs that you overhear between others. Record put downs that you hear on TV shows too. Bring your list to our next session.*

At the next session have the students take out their put-down surveys. Go around the room and have each student act out two items from his or her list, mimicking as closely as possible the method of delivery they witnessed when they observed the put down. To assure a broad sampling, instruct them to avoid repeating the substance of any previously shared put down. (If you have prepared the students adequately they will have numerous examples, since put downs are extremely common.) When everyone has had a turn to contribute, ask if there are any additional put downs that should be added to the list. Then go back and categorize and tally the examples. Here are three possible categories:

1. Reflex put downs (often an unconscious habit)
2. Teasing or joking put downs
3. Malicious (intentionally hurtful) put downs

Discuss the different motivations that lead to each type of put down, emphasizing that all types are often interpreted by the receiver as intentionally hurtful and can damage friendships.

Now ask the students to think of positive responses that could be substituted for habitual and joking put downs. Choose two or three put downs from those shared and brainstorm ways to change the wording or the object of the put down so that it is no longer hurtful.

Give the students a few minutes to write a positive substitute for at least two of the put downs on their 24-hour surveys. Go around the group and ask the students to share what they have written. Ask the students to act out the positive substitutes in the same way they did the put downs.

Discussion Questions:
— Where do we learn put downs?
— How do put-downs make people feel?
— What would be the effect on this group if we were always putting each other down?
— How should you respond to people who put you down?
— How can you break the habit of putting others down?
— How do positive, affirming statements make people feel?
— What would be the effect on this group if we said mostly positive, affirming things to each other?
— Why don't we say positive, affirming things more often?

Feeling Faces
Expressing Feelings with Masks

Objectives: The students will:
—identify a variety of feelings and associate them with feeling words
—recall and share incidents in which they experienced various feelings.

Materials: paper plates, flat wooden sticks (such as tongue depressors or popsicle sticks), scissors, colored markers and/or crayons, and glue

Procedure: Get the attention of the students and tell them to listen carefully while you read them the poem below. Ask the students to listen for feelings and to remember as many as they can.

Angry at Marty
Loving t'ward Lou
I'm full of feelings
What shall I do?

Proud of my drawing
Jealous of your bike
I show my feelings
And hide them, too

Happy after winning
Sad when I lose
I change my feelings
Like I change my shoes.

Tired in the morning
Hungry at noon
Do you have feelings
That bother you, too?

Depressed by grades
Scared of the dark
Why all these feelings...
What good do they do?

Surprised by mysteries
Amused by cartoons
If you lack feelings
I'll give some to you.

Excited by birthdays
Bored when they're through
I'll understand feelings
In a year or two.

After you have read the poem, ask the students to call out the feeling words that they identified. Point out that it is perfectly normal to experience all of the feelings mentioned and that, while everyone experiences them, each person feels and expresses them a little differently. Jot each word on the board and add others until you have a list that includes:

happy	sad	scared
angry	proud	excited
confused	tired	surprised
bored	amused	jealous
loving	hungry	depressed

Have the students pair up. Distribute one set of mask-making materials to each pair of students and, in your own words, explain:

You are going to work together as a team to create a mask that shows one of the feelings listed on the board. First, agree on the feeling you want to illustrate and then, using colored markers, make a face on the paper plate that depicts that feeling. Exaggerate the features to make the feeling come across as forcefully as possible.

Demonstrate the process, or show the students a mask that you have made in advance. Circulate and help the students as needed. Help young students cut eye holes in their masks and glue their sticks in place to create handles.

When the masks are finished, have each pair join three other pairs to form circles of eight. Direct the students to take turns holding their mask in front of their face, relating a time when they experienced the feeling shown, and acting out some of the things they did and said to express that feeling. Circulate and coach the students, as necessary, reminding them to pass their mask to their partner after they have had a turn so that their partner can have a turn also.

Suggest that the masks be displayed around the room and that the students continue to use them throughout the year to aid them in expressing feelings. Conclude the activity with a total group discussion.

Discussion Questions:

— Which feelings were easiest to express and recognize? Which were hardest? Why do you think that is?
— How did you feel when you were acting out your situation?
— Did the mask make it easier to act out your feelings? Why or why not?
— Why is it important to be aware of and express our feelings?
— Who decided how you would express your feeling? In real life, who always decides?
— Did partners who were expressing the same feeling always express them in the same way?
— When you have feelings that make it hard for you to work in school, what can you do to feel better? Whom can you talk to?

Variations:

- Make paper-bag masks, which require large eye holes but no gluing.
- If the group is relatively small, lead the sharing, dramatizations, and discussion in one large circle.
- If time is short, spread the activity over two sessions. Make the masks during the first session; lead the sharing, dramatizations, and discussion during the second.

Anatomy of Stress
Experience Sheet and Discussion

Objectives: The students will:
—associate stressors with familiar physiological responses.
—describe actions they can take to relieve stress symptoms when they occur.

Materials: one copy of the experience sheet, "Stress Alarm!" for each student

Procedure: Engage the students in a discussion about stress and stressors. Explain that a stressor is any thought, condition, or event that causes a person to become anxious, worried, tense, or upset.

Point out that the human body has strong physiological reactions when confronted with a stressor. Ask the students to name some of the sensations they've noticed in their own bodies when they are tense or worried. List these on the board.

Distribute the experience sheets and read through the directions aloud. Instruct the students to complete the graphic outline of the body (on the sheet) by illustrating the various reactions listed. For example, suggest that they draw big worried eyes; a tight, panting mouth; a tummy full of butterflies; jittery hands; expanded lungs; and anything else they can think of. Encourage the students to use symbols and to be as creative as possible.

Have them form groups of six and share their completed drawings. Then display the drawings around the room. Lead a follow-up discussion.

Discussion Questions:
— Why is it a good idea to know some of the reactions our bodies have to stress?
— What are some things you can do to relieve these feelings when they occur?
— What can you do if you start to feel anxious or worried, and are not sure why?
— If you feel worried or stressed at school who can you talk to?

Stress Alarm!
Experience Sheet

When you get scared or think you have a big problem, your BRAIN sends out signals that prepare your body to fight or to run. Follow the path through the maze of body reactions.

First, a chemical called adrenaline speeds up your body system, and then...

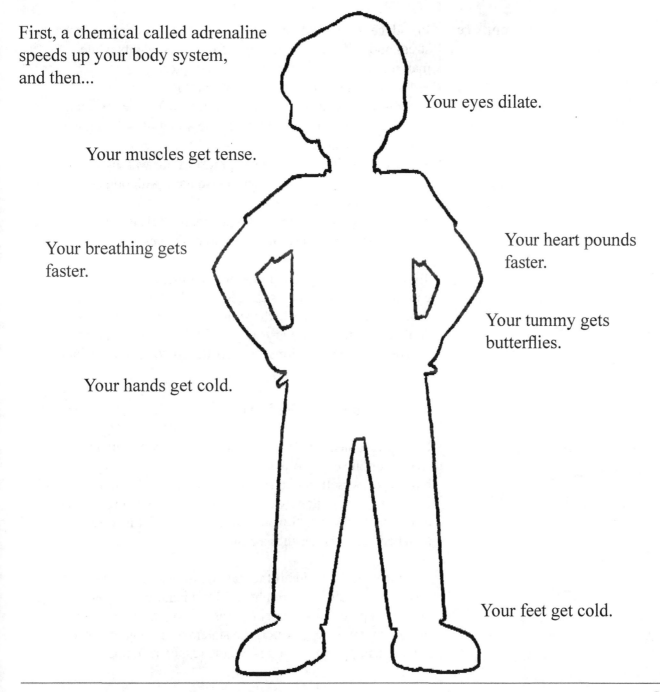

Your eyes dilate.

Your muscles get tense.

Your breathing gets faster.

Your heart pounds faster.

Your tummy gets butterflies.

Your hands get cold.

Your feet get cold.

Self-Talk and Stress
Discussion and Game

Objectives: The students will:
—state the importance of positive self-talk as an antidote to stress.
—describe the impact of self-talk on feelings and performance.

Materials: index cards listing stressful situations (see directions, below)

Procedure: Introduce this activity by discussing the connection between stress and self-talk. Invite input from the students while making these points and offering examples:
- Responses to stress come from within.
- Self-talk (the words we say to ourselves) serves as a major link between the things we believe about ourselves and our reactions to stress.
- We engage in self-talk during most of our waking moments.
- Self-talk is like a conversation we have with ourselves, often *about* ourselves.
- Whether we feel better or worse in stressful situations depends partly on what we say to ourselves.

To prepare for the game, think of a number of situations that commonly cause students to indulge in both positive and negative self-talk. Write the situations on index cards. (Use the situations listed on the next page, add different situations based on your own observations, and ask the students to contribute others.)

Place the cards in a pile, face down.

Have a volunteer draw a card and read aloud the situation written on the card. Ask what the volunteer might say to himself or herself in that situation. For example, upon realizing that an important homework assignment has been left at home, a student might say, "I would forget my head if it weren't attached" or "The teacher's going to kill me."

Ask the class to decide if the statement represents negative or positive self-talk. You might call for a hand signal, such as "thumbs up" if the statement is positive or "thumbs down" if the statement is negative. If the statement is negative, give the student an opportunity to restate the response in positive terms.

If the student has difficulty, ask the class to assist. For example, the student could say, "I forgot my homework today, but I am getting better at remembering my homework and other things. I have a good memory."

Continue until all of the cards have been drawn. Involve as many students as possible. Conduct a brief class discussion at the conclusion of the game.

Discussion Questions:
— What differences did you notice between how you *felt* when your thoughts were positive and negative?
— What do you find easiest about controlling self-talk? What do you find hardest?
— What ideas do you have for getting control of your self-talk?

Situations:
- You forget to bring your homework to school.
- You get 4 out of 10 wrong on a spelling test.
- You get 9 out of 10 right on a quiz.
- You miss the school bus.
- You are left out of a game on the playground.
- You strike out in a softball game.
- You move to a new neighborhood.
- Your best friend goes shopping with someone else.
- You arrive late to class.
- You get an A on an assignment.
- A group project goes well.
- Your new haircut didn't turn out like you wanted it to.
- You spill your milk at lunch.
- You have a library book that is six weeks overdue.
- You run for student council and lose.
- You run for student council and win.
- Someone points out that you have a stain on your shirt.
- You have to complete a lengthy report on the civil war.
- You get a B- on your book report.
- You are asked to baby-sit.

First Feelings
Experience Sheet and Discussion

Objectives: The students will:
—learn and practice acceptable ways to express negative emotions.
—identify feelings that typically precede/precipitate anger and identify ways to deal with them.

Materials: one copy of the experience sheet, "Dealing with Anger" for each student, whiteboard

Procedure: Write the heading, "Anger" on the board. Ask the class to brainstorm specific examples of angry behavior. List them beneath the heading. Then ask the students to describe how their bodies feel when they are angry, and talk briefly about the power of the emotion.

Read the following scenario to the class:

Desiree skipped out of her classroom happily. On her way home she boasted to her friend, Antonio, "All I have to do for homework is math, and it's a cinch. Math is my easiest subject. I always get A's." She ran into her house and threw down her backpack. Off she ran to play with friends until dinner. That evening she played games with her sister and watched some television, forgetting to do her homework. The next day in school, when her teacher asked for her Math homework, Desiree looked startled and then turned red. "I forgot to do it," she said, looking down at her backpack. As she looked up, Antonio was watching her from across the room. Desiree suddenly stuck her tongue out at him and wouldn't look at him for the rest of the morning. At recess she refused to play ball with Antonio and told him she was mad at him.

Following the story, facilitate discussion by asking these questions:
— What were Desiree's first feelings when she realized that she had forgotten her homework?
— How could she have expressed those feelings?
— How did Desiree feel when she saw her friend Antonio watching her?

— Why did she refuse to play with Antonio at recess?
— How could Desiree have expressed her feelings toward Antonio?
— What could she have done to control her behavior toward her friend?

Make the following points in a discussion about anger:
- Anger is a normal emotion. We all get angry and need to learn acceptable and effective ways to deal with anger.
- Anger tends to be a secondary feeling or emotion. In other words, one or more other feelings usually precede anger. For example, when Desiree realized she had forgotten to do her homework, her first emotions may have been shock, humiliation, panic, regret, and desperation in rapid succession.
- Another example: When a student fails a test for which she or he studied hard, the first feelings are overwhelming disappointment and frustration. But anger follows so quickly that it's the only emotion the rest of the class observes. The same thing happens with other feelings, too.
- Other people usually have difficulty coping with someone's anger. This is partly because anger acts as a mask, hiding what is really going on. Others will have a much easier time responding to your frustration, grief, relief, sadness, or fear than to your anger. Consequently, a very valuable skill to develop is the skill of expressing your initial feelings, rather than just your anger.
- Anger puts stress on the body. Too much anger experienced too often can lead to illness.

Distribute the experience sheet, "Dealing with Anger." Go over the directions and give the students a few minutes to respond to the questions individually.

Have the students form small groups. Ask them to discuss the situations and their responses to the questions.

Discussion Questions:

— What did you decide were Marco's first emotions? Jed's? Nieko's?
— How could each character have expressed his or her first emotions?
— What other behaviors did you come up with in each situation?
— How does anger mask what is really going on?
— Why is anger such a difficult emotion to deal with in other people?
— If you have difficulty dealing with anger, what can you do to get help?

Extension:

Have volunteers role play several of the best alternatives suggested in each situation.

Dealing with Anger
Experience Sheet

Situation 1:

Marco and Jed were best buddies. After school, they often stayed on the playground to play their favorite game, basketball. During one game, as they were passing the ball back and forth, Marco suddenly spotted his dog running loose across the playground. "Here, Rambo," he shouted, as Jed slammed the ball his way. Marco felt the impact of the rapidly flying ball right on the side of his face, and fell to the ground. After rubbing his stinging face and catching his breath, Marco got up and started screaming at Jed. "Hey, you did that on purpose, you jerk." With tears streaming down his face, he ran toward his friend swinging his fists and shouting, "I am gonna get you back!" Backing away, Jed yelled, "It's your own fault, dummy. You weren't watching the ball!"

Questions:

What were Marco's first feelings after
he fell to the ground?

_____

_____

_____

_____

How did he express those feelings?

_____

_____

How could he have better expressed those feelings?

_____

_____

_____

Situation 2:

Mieko had been attending gymnastics class in the evenings at the local gymnasium. She liked to do tumbling and easily performed handsprings, cartwheels, and flips. However, when it was her turn to work on the balance beam, Mieko didn't do all of the movements easily. One evening, Mieko was practicing turns on the beam and kept falling off. She just couldn't keep her balance. After practice, when Mieko's coach asked her to stay for a few minutes so he could give her some tips on how to keep her balance, she picked up her things and stormed out of the gym, slamming the door behind her. "He's just picking on me," Mieko grumbled as she stomped down the street.

Questions:

What were Mieko's first feelings when the coach asked her to stay after practice?

_____

_____

How did she express those feelings?

_____

_____

_____

How could she have better expressed those feelings?

_____

_____

_____

_____

What Makes Me Angry
Experience Sheet and Discussion

Objectives: | The students will:
—examine people, conditions, and situations that generate anger in them.
—describe appropriate ways to handle or express anger.

Materials: | one copy of the experience sheet, "Things I Get Angry About," for each student

Procedure: | Begin by involving the students in a brief dialogue on the subject of anger. For example, you might write the word *anger* on the board and ask, "Has anyone felt this emotion today?" allowing two or three volunteers to briefly describe what happened to make them angry. Or you might ask the students to think of other words that describe different levels of anger (irritated, annoyed, furious, etc.), list them, and then talk about how anger builds.

Next, distribute the experience sheets. Ask the students to think about and write down various conditions, situations, and people that cause them anger. Instruct the students to list one or two appropriate ways of handling the anger in each situation.

In a follow-up discussion, invite several volunteers to share one item from their list. Invite the other students to suggest additional ways to handle anger in each of those situations. In the process, make the following points about anger:
- Anger is a basic human emotion and is neither bad nor good.
- Sometimes anger serves a protective function.
- There are healthy and appropriate ways to deal with the anger we feel.
- Each of us is responsible for our own feelings and behavior.
- It is how we react to a situation, not the situation itself, that causes our anger and upset.

Discussion Questions: | 1. How does your body feel when you are angry?
2. How can you tell when someone else is angry?
3. Why is it a good idea to find positive ways of dealing with anger?
4. What have you learned about handling anger from this activity?

Things I Get Angry About
Experience Sheet

Many people react angrily to the same things—and the same people—over and over again. What about you? Are there certain things (such as not getting your way or not being listened to) that almost always upset you? List several people and situations that usually make you angry. Then list several things you can do to deal with your feelings of anger.

Situations and People	What I Can Do About My Anger

Taking Control of Anger
Brainstorming Discussion and Experience Sheet

Objectives: The students will:
—brainstorm strategies for managing anger.
—select and think through six preferred anger management strategies.

Materials: one experience sheet, "Six Strategies for Controlling Anger," for each student; scissors, tape, pencils, crayons, colored markers; colored construction paper precut to form cards 3-1/2 x 5 inches in size.

Procedure: Ask the students to think about a time that they were really mad and yet were able to calm down and get their anger under control. Ask:

— *What helped you to calm down?*

On the board or chart paper, record the calming strategies suggested by the students. If they are not mentioned, add the following:

- Take several deep breaths.
- Count to 10.
- Distract yourself by doing something fun.
- Share your feelings with an adult or friend you trust.
- Do something active like ride a bike, hit a baseball or tennis ball, jog, or dance.
- Imagine a peaceful place.
- Quietly talk to yourself until you calm down.
- Write down both sides of the problem and think it through.
- Listen to your favorite music.
- Physically remove yourself from the situation. Walk away.
- Remind yourself of the consequences of out-of-control anger.

Distribute the experience sheets. Have the students choose their top six strategies of managing anger and illustrate them in the squares on the experience sheet. Suggest that they choose from the brainstormed list, and add other ideas as well. Provide pencils, crayons and markers.

Distribute scissors, construction paper cards and glue. Have the students cut out their illustrated strategies and glue them to construction paper cards, leaving a boarder all the way around.

Have the children take turns sharing their cards. Use some of the discussion questions to stimulate discussion during the sharing period.

Discussion Questions:
— In what kinds of situations will this strategy work best?
— How well has this strategy worked when you've used it before?
— What kinds of things cause kids to get angry?
— What kinds of things provoke anger in adults?
— What happens when anger gets out of control?
— What are some examples of justifiable anger?
— When anger is justifiable, is it less threatening? Why or why not?

Variations:
When everyone has had a turn sharing, give the students a few minutes to mingle and negotiate trades.

Six Strategies for Controlling Anger
Experience Sheet

In the six boxes, illustrate and label your top six strategies for calming down when you are angry. Use symbols and drawings.

#1	#2
#3	#4
#5	#6

Relaxation Three Ways
Deep Breathing, Meditation, and Muscle Relaxation

Objectives:

The students will:
— learn and practice three relaxation techniques.
— understand the purpose of each technique.
— compare the relative benefits of the three techniques.

Materials:

reasonable space and moveable chairs; optional soft instrumental music

Procedure:

The essence of stress reduction is relaxation. You can repeatedly urge mindfulness and relaxation, explaining in detail their value, but until you actually teach and routinely practice methods to accomplish these objectives — prior to tests, following breaks, as transitions from active to quiet tasks — nothing much will change. These three relaxation techniques are provided because they are easy to teach and highly effective.

Provided here are three distinct methods of achieving relaxation. Each is simple, easy to learn, and effective. The key to success is repetition. Have your students practice one or more of these exercises regularly - prior to tests, following breaks, as transitions from active to quiet tasks. Make relaxation part of their routine. After the children have experienced the different relaxation methods, use the questions below to spark a discussion.

Discussion Questions:

— Which of the three relaxation exercises did you like best? Why?
— Which exercise was most effective in helping you to relax?
— Which exercise are you most apt to use on your own?
— During the meditation, how difficult was it to concentrate on counting?
— During the muscle relaxation exercise, where did you feel the most tension?
— During what part of your day are you usually very relaxed? When are you usually very tense?
— Which of these techniques could you use to relax during the tense part of your day?

Deep Breathing

The simplest, most direct route to relaxation is that of deep breathing. Explain to the children that when they are tense, nervous, angry, or excited, their breathing becomes more rapid. Deliberately slowing and controlling the depth and rate of their breathing can help them to calm down and feel more relaxed.

Read the directions slowly, progressing from chest to abdominal (belly) breathing and then combining the movements in one slow, continuous four-count exercise.

Chest-breathing

Sit in a comfortable position and close your eyes.
Inhale and exhale deeply through your nose three times.
Place your left hand on your stomach, just below your ribs. Place your right hand on your chest.
Breathe normally and notice where your breath is coming from.
Now take a long, slow, deep breath into your chest. Your right hand will rise while your left hand remains fairly still.
Pause briefly, keeping your chest full, then exhale slowly through your nose.
Repeat this "chest breathing" three times.
Breathe in, hold, release... breathe in, hold, release... breathe in, hold, release.
Breathe normally.

Belly-breathing

Now, take a long, slow deep breath into your stomach. Your left hand will rise, while your right hand remains fairly still.
Pause briefly, feeling your stomach muscles push up, then exhale slowly through your nose.
Repeat this "belly breathing" three times.
Breathe in, hold, release... breathe in, hold, release... breathe in, hold, release.
Breathe normally.

Combined chest-belly breathing

Count one: breathe into your belly (left hand rises)
Count two: breathe into your chest (right hand rises)
Count three: Exhale from your belly (left hand lowers)
Count four: Exhale from your chest (right hand lowers)
Pause.
Repeat: one... two... three... four...
Continue for 2-3 minutes.

5-Minute Meditation

Explain to the children that the purpose of meditation is to relax the body and quiet the mind. Point out that our bodies are usually active and moving. Even while sitting, we tend to shift, turn, and twitch. Similarly, our minds never stop producing thoughts, not even during sleep. By sitting quietly for a few minutes while breathing naturally and focusing all of our attention on a particular sound, we can calm both mind and body.

In this exercise the children will focus on the sound of their own voice counting from one to four. Have the children move their chairs to create maximum distance from one another. If possible, they should face blank walls, or at least face away from other children. A circle, with everyone turned to face out, works well. Tell the children to count very quietly, just above a whisper.

Slowly read these directions:

> *Sit straight in your chair. Fold your hands in your lap or rest them on your thighs.*
> *Look down slightly with your eyes, keeping your head straight.*
> *Sit quietly and try not to move. Breathe naturally.*

Pause briefly, then continue...

> *Focus your attention on your breathing.*
> *Silently count "one" as you inhale. Count "two" as you exhale. Count "three" as you inhale. Count "four" as you exhale.*
> *Continue breathing in and out with each count up to ten.*
> *Start over, breathing and counting up to ten.*
> *Concentrate on the sound of your own voice counting. If other thoughts enter your mind, that's okay. Just let them pass and go back to focusing on your voice.*
> *Continue for 5 minutes.*

Progressive Muscle Relaxation

One of the best ways to differentiate a tense muscle from a relaxed one, thereby guaranteeing relaxation, is to first exaggerate the tension. Progressive muscle relaxation helps children feel the difference by tensing and relaxing one muscle group at a time, from toe to head. As you read the directions, exaggerate your inflexion to convey the alternate sensations of tension and relaxation. Play the role of coach.

Sit or lie in a comfortable position with your eyes closed. Breathe naturally.

Think about each set of muscles as I tell you to tense and hold for 5 seconds. Try to move only the muscles I tell you to move, keeping the rest of your body still. Notice how it feels. Then notice the difference when I tell you to relax those muscles.

Tense your toes by flexing them as though you were standing on tiptoe. Hold. Relax.

Flex your ankles and move them around in circles. Flex again. Hold. Relax.

Tense and stretch your calf muscles by pushing hard with your heels. Hold. Relax.

Tense the large muscles in your thighs. Hold. Relax.

Tense your hip and buttocks muscles. Feel your hips lift. Hold. Relax.

Tense your abdominal muscles. Feel them tighten. Hold. Relax.

Tense your stomach muscles. Suck them in as tightly as you can. Hold. Relax.

Make tight fists with your fingers. Tighter. Hold. Relax.

Flex your wrists. Make circles with your wrists. Flex again. Hold. Relax.

Tense the muscles in your arms. Make your arms as stiff as boards. Hold. Relax.

Tense your shoulder muscles. Hunch your shoulders up to your ears. Hold. Relax.

Tense your neck by touching your chin to your collarbone. Hold. Relax.

Turn your neck as far as it will go to the right. Hold. Relax.

Turn your neck as far as it will go to the left. Hold. Relax.

Scrunch all the muscles of your face as tightly as you can. Hold. Relax.

Now tense your whole body, starting with your toes all the way up to your face. Hold. Relax.

Something That Causes Me Stress
A Sharing Circle

Objectives:

The students will:
—identify stressors in their lives.
—describe feelings and sensations associated with stress.
—name specific ways of dealing with stress.

Introduce the Topic.

Our topic for this session is, "Something That Causes Me Stress." Do you ever get tongue tied? Feel uptight or on edge? Get a headache or a queasy stomach when you're not sick? Chances are the cause of those feelings is stress. Many different things can cause stress — worrying about a test, feeling angry at someone, or not getting enough sleep, for example. Even good things can cause stress — like the excitement of waiting for a special event. Think of something that causes you stress and tell us about it. What happens to cause the stress, and how does it affect the way you feel, the thoughts you have, and the things you do? Take a few minutes to think about it. The topic is, "Something That Causes Me Stress."

Discussion Questions:

— Do the same kinds of things frequently cause you stress?
— If you know something is likely to stress you, what can you do about it?
— Do feelings of stress do us any good? Explain your answer.

I Succeeded Because I Encouraged Myself
A Sharing Circle

Objectives:

The students will:

—identify a personal success.

—describe how self-encouragement helps promote success.

Introduce the topic:

Our topic for this session is, "I Succeeded Because I Encouraged Myself." Have you ever wanted to do something and weren't quite sure you could? Think of a time when you felt unsure, but encouraged yourself and, consequently, found a way to be successful. Perhaps you tried to teach your pet a trick, or needed to do a good job on a report for school. Maybe you were trying to master something on a computer, or were learning a new game. Whatever it was, you were not sure you could do it, but after giving yourself some encouraging words, you were successful. Take a few quiet moments to think it over. The topic is, "I Succeeded Because I Encouraged Myself."

Discussion Questions:

— What do you think caused each of you to be successful?

— What kinds of doubts did you have to overcome to be successful?

— What do you think would have happened if you had used discouraging words instead of encouraging words?

One of My Best Habits
A Sharing Circle

Objectives: The students will identify and describe positive habits they have developed.

Introduce the topic: *In our circle today, we're going to talk about good habits we've developed. The topic is, "One of My Best Habits." What good habits do you have? Maybe you do something every single day for your health, like brush your teeth. Or maybe you have the good habit of always making sure you are on time for school and other places you are supposed to be. Perhaps you make it a habit to do things to keep your life organized and smooth-running, like putting your things where they belong at home. Tell us about any good habit that you have developed. Let's think about it for a moment. Then, when you are ready to share, raise your hand. The topic is, "One of My Best Habits."*

Discussion Questions:
— How do good habits cause us to feel about ourselves?
— Did you get any ideas for good habits you'd like to start developing in yourself?
— You don't have to tell us what it is, but did you realize that you might have a bad habit or two that you'd like to change?

Something I'd Like To Do Better
A Sharing Circle

Objectives: The students will identify and describe areas in which they need to improve.

Introduce the topic: *Our topic for this session is, "Something I'd Like To Do Better." In our circle today, we are going to tell each other about a skill or ability that we would like to improve. Think of something that you are not as good at as you would like to be. It might be some area of your school work. It might be in sports or an area of recreation. It might be the way in which you get along with members of your family or with friends. Think about it for a minute or two before we begin to share. Our circle topic is, "Something I'd Like To Do Better."*

Discussion Questions:
— Which was harder to talk about, yesterday's topic on things you do well, or today's topic on things you don't do as well as you'd like to? Why?
— How were we different or the same in the things they want to improve?
— Why is it important to identify the areas in which we need to improve?

I Almost Got Into a Fight
A Sharing Circle

Objectives: The students will describe methods they used to prevent conflict situations from becoming fights.

Introduce the topic: *Our topic for this session is, "I Almost Got Into a Fight!" From time to time each of us has a disagreement or conflict with another person. Sometimes conflicts aren't very serious, and sometimes they are. Can you think of a time when something happened between you and someone else that almost caused you to get into a fight? Maybe you wanted to fight because you were upset. Or maybe the other person tried to start the fight. Perhaps you both felt like fighting, but then, somehow, you settled the problem peacefully. Tell us how the incident happened, and how you felt, but please don't tell us who the other person was. The topic is, "I Almost Got Into a Fight."*

Discussion Questions:
— Is conflict always bad, or can it sometimes lead to good things?
— What were the main ways we kept these disagreements or conflicts from becoming big fights?
— Is fighting a good way to resolve conflict? Why or why not?

I Made a Plan and Followed Through

A Sharing Circle

Objectives:	The students will describe a goal that was reached through planning and follow-through.
Introduce the topic:	*Our topic for today is, "I Made a Plan and Followed Through." Think of a time when there was something you really wanted to do, and it required some planning on your part. You may have wanted a bike or a stereo, and had to save money to help pay for it. Or maybe you wanted very much to pass a test , or get an "A" in a class—and to do it, you had to plan a study schedule. Possibly you wanted to surprise someone with a party or a gift, and you had to prepare carefully to create the surprise. Whatever it was—your plan succeeded. Take a few moments to think of such a time before we share. The topic is, "I Made a Plan and Followed Through."*
Discussion Questions:	— What was similar about our plans? — Why do we sometimes need help to carry out our plans? — What do you think would have happened if no one had made a plan? — How was it helpful to hear about all these plans that succeeded?

Additional Sharing Circle Topics

How I React When I'm Angry

A Time I Couldn't Control My Curiosity

Someone Who Respects My Feelings

A Time I Handled My Feelings Well

I Could Have Hurt Someone's Feelings, But Didn't

A Feeling I Had a Hard Time Accepting

A Time I Was Alone But Not Lonely

A Thought I Have That Makes Me Feel Happy

I Did Something Impulsive and Regretted It Later

A Time I Really Controlled My Feelings

A Time I Was Afraid to Do Something But Did It Anyway

A Way I Get Over Being Afraid

I Did Something for My Body and It Improved My Spirit

Something I Worried About That Turned Out Okay

A Time I Felt a Lot of Tension and Stress

Something I Do for My Own Well Being

Someone I Can Talk to When I'm Worried

My Favorite Physical Exercise

Where I Go When I Want to Be Alone

A Way I Take Care of My Body

What I Say When I Talk to Myself

A Way I've Learned to Calm Myself Down

Music That Makes Me Feel Good

A Time I Felt Upset and Didn't Know Why

Social Awareness

Working Together
Discussion and Experience Sheet

Objectives:	The students will: —define the word *cooperate*. —describe the benefits of cooperating with others to achieve a goal.
Materials:	one copy of the experience sheet, "Together Is Better" for each student; whiteboard
Procedure:	Write the word *cooperate* on the board. Ask the students what it means to cooperate with another person. Accept all contributions, jotting key words and phrases on the board. Attempt to agree upon a simple definition of the word.

Remind the students of specific occasions when you have asked groups of two or more to work together to complete a task or assignment. Ask them to think carefully about what they accomplished and how they went about it. Then ask, "What did you gain by working together cooperatively?"

Again, accept all contributions. Through questions and discussion, help the students identify the following potential benefits of working cooperatively with another person:
* When people work together, they save time.
* When people work together, they think of more solutions to a problem.
* When people work together, their solutions are more creative.
* When people work together, they have fun.
* When people work together, they do a better job.

Distribute the experience sheets. After going over the directions, give the students a few minutes to complete the sheet. When the students have completed both sides of their experience sheets have them move into small groups of 3 or 4 and share what they have written. Facilitate a culminating class discussion.

Discussion Questions:

— What are some ways that you cooperate with others at home?
— Why is it important to cooperate when working with others?
— What happens when one person in a group is uncooperative?
— If you had an uncooperative person in your group, what could you do?

Together Is Better
Experience Sheet

In the space below, write two or three sentences that describe what cooperating means to you. Below are some words that you might want to use. Use other words, too.

share	**compromise**	**help**
team	**win**	**think**
together	**work**	**laugh**
listen	**enjoy**	**accomplish**
talk	**support**	**agree**

Cooperating means... _____

_____

_____

_____

_____

_____

_____

Now use the back of this paper, and write about a time when you cooperated with someone to accomplish a goal, instead of working alone.

_____

Cooperating With Others
Self-Assessment and Group Task

Objectives:

The students will:
—assess their attitudes and behaviors in group situations.
—describe the qualities and abilities they bring to groups.
—list the most important qualities of a group member.

Materials:

one copy of the self-assessment, "The Group and I," for each student; writing materials; several samples of want ads (optional)

Procedure:

Distribute the self-assessments. Explain to the students that you want them to take a few minutes to evaluate the attitudes and behaviors they have in groups. Answer any questions about procedure and then give the students 5 to 10 minutes to complete the assessment. When the students are finished, assure them that the contents of their self-assessments are private. Ask them to take a few moments to review what they have written, and then fold the sheets over or put them away.

Have the students form groups of four to six. Ask them to think of one thing that they learned from completing the self-assessment that they wouldn't mind sharing with their group. Allow time for sharing.

When they have finished sharing, tell the groups that you want them to work together to write a "want ad" for a newmember for their group. (If you have ad samples, give one to each group.) Tell the groups to list in their ad the most important qualifications a group member should have. Explain that the qualities and abilities they list should be of benefit to almost any kind of group.

When the groups have finished, ask them to share their ads with the rest of the class. Facilitate a class discussion.

Discussion Question:

— What are the most important qualities/ abilities a person can bring to a group? Why are they so important?
— How can a group bring out the best in each of its members?
— Do members of a group always have to agree? Why or why not?
— What can you do when disagreements and conflict erupt in a group?

The Group and I
Self-Assessment

How do you feel about cooperating with others? What are your actions?
Read each set of statements. Put an **X** on the line to show how you rate yourself.

I usually avoid group activities.	—————————┼—————————	I take part in group activities as often as possible.
I'm never the first person to start a conversation.	—————————┼—————————	I go out of my way to start conversations with other people.
I prefer to be alone.	—————————┼—————————	I try to be with other people.
When I'm in a group, I don't say much.	—————————┼—————————	I contribute a lot to every group I'm with.
I am not an important group member.	—————————┼—————————	My membership in a group is always important.

Think of a time when you helped a group accomplish its goal. List the three most
important qualities or abilities you brought to the group.

1. _____

2. _____

3. _____

Reaching Out
Stories and Discussion

Objectives: The students will:
— recognize and describe the feelings of others.
— demonstrate understanding of the needs of people who are different from themselves.
— recognize that all people, including those who are culturally and physically different from one another, share the same kinds of feelings.

Materials: writing materials for older students; art materials for younger students

Procedure: Choose one (or more) of the following stories and read it to the students. In your own words, say: *I'm going to read you a short story. I'd like your help in thinking of some solutions to the problem that the person in the story is experiencing.*

After reading the story, facilitate a class discussion using the questions provided. Focus on helping your students identify and understand the feelings of the children in the story, *from their point of view.* Explain to the students that this kind of understanding is called *empathy* — the ability to "feel with" another person.

After the discussion, ask each student to write his or her own ending to the story (or to one of the stories, if you read several). If your students are very young, you may prefer to have them draw a picture illustrating a positive conclusion. Ask the students to share their story endings or illustrations with the class.

Jamil's First Day of School

Jamil entered his first-grade classroom as a non-English speaker, having just arrived from the Philippines. He had never been in a school before and, on his first day, he began running around the classroom making noises. When the teacher told him to sit down, he didn't understand what she said and continued to make silly humming sounds. The other children began to laugh and started to make noises, too. The teacher scolded the children, and said that they would have to give up 5 minutes of their recess to discuss their behavior. During the discussion, the teacher explained that Jamil did not understand English and never learned appropriate school behavior. She asked the children to help Jamil become a successful school citizen.

Discussion Questions:

— How do you think Jamil felt being a new boy in the class?
— How do you think Jamil felt not understanding what anyone said?
— What could you do to help Jamil understand good school behavior?
— What could Jamil have done to help the other children learn about his life in the Philippines?
— How could you be Jamil's friend and help him learn English words?

Karla's Ordeal

Nine-year-old Karla tried to make friends at every school she attended, and this was the third school in the past year. But the other girls made fun of her old clothes and sometimes unbrushed hair and dirty face. Karla lived with her dad and two brothers in an old camper. They moved from one trailer park to another, in whatever town her father could find work. The camper had no running water, so Karla had to use the trailer-park bathrooms, which sometimes had neither showers nor hot water. At school, the children called her "Homeless Orphan" on the playground. "I am not homeless. I live in a trailer with my dad, who calls me his princess," Karla would answer. Finally, one of the older girls, overhearing the name-calling, shouted to the others, "Come on. Quit teasing Karla. She's the best artist in the school. I saw her pictures on the cafeteria bulletin board!"

Discussion Questions:

— How do you think Karla felt when the other girls teased her?
— Why do you think the older girl tried to defend Karla by shouting to the ones who were teasing her?
— What could Karla have done to try to make friends with the girls who were teasing her?
— What could the other girls have done to help Karla when she came to school with a dirty face?

Why Jerome Won't Talk

Jerome loved attending Scouts when they played outdoor games, made things out of wood or paper, or went hiking. He could run fast, catch balls, and make things with his hands better than most of the other boys. But when it came time to say the Scout promise or join in group discussions, Jerome wouldn't participate. Every time he tried to speak, he began to stutter, "I p-p-p-promise to d-d-do..." Jerome usually quit before he finished a sentence. Often, some of the boys put their hands over their mouths and giggled. Jerome saw this and he stopped even trying to speak. The Scout leader tried to encourage him to speak, "Come on, Jerome. Keep trying. It doesn't have to be perfect." But Jerome just looked down, silently.

Discussion Questions:

— How do you think Jerome felt about stuttering when he talked?
— How do you think Jerome felt when the boys giggled?
— What could the boys have done to help him?
— What could Jerome have done to make friends with the boys?

A Test of Friendship

Naomi and Lisa became good friends in the sixth grade. They were in the same class at school and lived in apartment buildings on the same city block. The girls took violin lessons together after school and played on the neighborhood soccer team. They often slept over at each other's apartments, and sometimes ate dinner with each other's families. The only problems the girls encountered in their friendship occurred on holidays, especially during the winter. Naomi was Jewish and celebrated holy days with her family, at home and in the synagogue. During Hanukkah in December, Naomi wanted to stay home with her family to light the candles on their menorah and play games with the dreidl. Lisa wanted Naomi to spend the night with her and decorate her family's Christmas tree. The girls had a big argument over this, which almost ruined their friendship.

Discussion Questions:

— How do you think the girls could have solved their problem?
— What could the girls' families have done to help them solve their problem?
— How could the girls have used their differences to strengthen their friendship?

Recognizing the Needs of Others
Experience Sheets and Discussion

Objectives: The students will:
—understand the importance of empathy and how empathy is achieved.
—umpathize with people in a variety of situations.

Materials: one copy of the experience sheets, "Empathy Is…" and "Empathy Practice," for each student

Procedure: Give a copy of the experience sheet, "Empathy Is…," to each student. Tell the students that they have 3 minutes to translate the Braille sentence at the top of the sheet. Call time and have the students stop working. Ask:
— *Did anyone complete the translation? If so, what does the sentence say?*

Call on volunteers to read their translations, If no one was able to translate the sentence in the allotted time (which is likely), acknowledge the difficulty of the task and write the correct translation on the board. (Translation: *Empathy is imagining yourself in another person's shoes and feeling what they feel.*)

Have the students write the correct translation in the space provided on the bottom of the experience sheet. Ask:
—*How did you feel when you could not easily understand what you were reading?*

Encourage sharing. The point being to get the children to get in touch with their feelings and then to transpose those feelings to how others might feel in situations where they are unsure.

Call on volunteers. Discuss the similarity between the situation they faced with the Braille and the experience of a child who must adjust to a new culture with an unfamiliar language, or a child with a disability learning to perform a difficult skill. Ask:
—*Did this experience help you empathize with the child who can't speak English, or the child who is physically challenged by a disability?*

Talk about what it means to empathize with another person. Differentiate empathy from sympathy. Empathy is not feeling sorry for someone. Empathy is identifying with the person, feeling what they feel. For most people, empathy is not a well-developed response. Sometimes it requires conscious thought. Explain that the children may have to ask themselves, "What is this person feeling right now?" and "How would I feel in her situation?"

Read the Empathy Situations below to the students. After each one, ask the listed questions and call on volunteers to name their projected feelings. Write these on the board. Use their answers to generate discussion. For example, if a child says he would feel protective and angry as the parent of the immigrant child (first situation), ask "Why?" or "What thoughts led you to that conclusion?" Encourage the students to put themselves in the shoes of the various people—to really "get inside" their heads and hearts.

Empathy Situations

1. Luce is a new student at your school. She dresses differently from the other girls. Her clothes fit poorly and are not stylish. When the kids make fun of her and call her names, Luce tells her parents. Her father visits the school to find out what is going on. How would you feel if you were 1) Luce, 2) Luce's father, 3) the school principal?

2. Marcie Brown and her children buy a house on a large lot next to a big apartment complex. They discover that the apartments' drainage ditch crosses the back of their property. They want the drainage ditch moved so that they can build a pool, but the city says that the apartment complex can keep their drainage ditch where it is because it was built when their property was just an empty lot, giving the apartment complex what is called a "prescriptive easement." How would you feel if you were 1) Marcie Brown, 2) the owner of the apartment complex, 3) Marcie Brown's kids (who probably won't get a pool)?

3. Your city plans to demolish several blocks of old hotels and low-income apartment houses to build a new baseball stadium. Several hundred people will lose their homes. While the owners of the buildings will be paid by the city, the renters won't get anything. They band together and try to stop the city from building the ballpark. How would you feel if you were 1) a renter in danger of losing your home, 2) the owner of one of the condemned buildings, 3) the developer of the baseball stadium, 4) the city mayor, 5) a baseball fan?

4. Kim and Tracey have been best friends for years. One day Susan moves in next door to Kim and the two girls quickly become inseparable. Tracey tries to make it a threesome, but finds herself left out much of the time. How would you feel if you were 1) Tracey, 2) Kim, 3) Susan?

5. Jermane spends hours in the library researching the Lewis and Clark expedition for a written report. He gets a B. His friend Donovan downloads a report from the Internet and gets an A. Jermane complains to his mom who, against Jermane's wishes, tells the teacher. How would you feel if you were 1) Jermane, 2) Jermane's mother, 3) the teacher, 4) Donovan?

Give a copy of the experience sheet, "Empathy Practice," to each student. Go over the directions. Announce that for one week, you want them to watch and listen for feelings. Point out that feelings are a lot more difficult to notice than physical things like how someone looks. Suggest that the students be alert for situations that involve some sort of problem or conflict, like the ones you read to them earlier.

When the students bring in their completed sheets, have them take turns reporting what they observed. Go around the group and discuss one situation from each student. Then repeat the circuit as time allows.

Discussion Questions:

— What is the most difficult thing about being empathetic?
— What kinds of feelings were easier to discern, positive feelings or negative feelings? Why do you think that is?
— Why is having empathy important?
— Would you rather have friends who empathize with what you feel, or friends who don't seem to notice? Why?

Empathy Is...
Experience Sheet

The Braille Alphabet

A	B	C	D	E	F	G	H	I	J	K	L	M
N	O	P	Q	R	S	T	U	V	W	X	Y	Z

Using the Braille alphabet above, translate the following sentence. (Each word is separately underlined.)

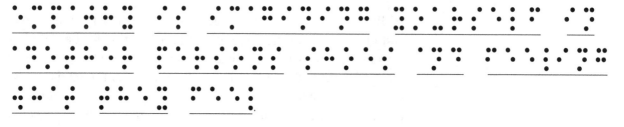

Write your translation here:

_____

_____

_____

_____

_____

Empathy Practice
Experience Sheet

For one week, notice situations in which people have strong feelings. Write down what was going on. Then try to empathize with each of the people involved. Write down what you think they feel.

Situation:	Feelings

Dare to Care
Dramatizations

Objectives: The students will:
—discuss ways of demonstrating empathy and caring.
—practice empathic, caring behaviors in a variety of dramatized scenarios.

Materials: whiteboard; found materials for props (optional)

Procedure: Explain to the students that there are many ways to demonstrate empathy and caring. Ask the students to think about ways in which they can show care and concern for other people. Generate a list of words and phrases that describe ways of caring and write them on the board. Here are some suggestions:

- listening
- cheering up someone
- helping
- volunteering
- inviting
- sharing
- smiling
- patting
- acknowledging
- thanking
- greeting new students
- accompanying
- hugging
- shaking hands
- thinking about your actions and their consequences
- treating others fairly
- giving presents
- singing to someone
- writing to a friend.

Discuss possible role-play situations using one of the words or phrases on the list. For example, the word volunteering could generate these scenarios:

- A teacher introduces a new student and asks if someone would show her around the school and help her set up her desk during the next recess. A student raises his hand to volunteer and does the job.

- A child, noticing that mom is very tired from working all day, volunteers to set the table for dinner and clear the table afterwards.

Discuss the possible actions and dialogue that might take place in each scenario. Then model the role-playing process by choosing volunteers to act out each scenario.

Divide the class into small groups and have each group choose one of the words from the board. Tell the groups to develop two or three scenarios that, when acted out, will effectively demonstrate that caring behavior. Have them assign a group member to each role, and then practice the scenario, making sure that every person has at least one part to play. Ask the students to repeat this procedure for each scenario they develop.

When the groups are finished practicing, invite them to dramatize their scenarios for the rest of the class. After each group is finished, discuss that group's dramatizations before going on to the next group. Ask, "How did these situations demonstrate the value of caring?"

Following all of the dramatizations, facilitate a culminating discussion.

Discussion Questions:

— How do you know how another person feels?
— Did feeling empathy for the other person in your scenario help you decide how to show caring?
— What is empathy and how do you know when you've got it?
— How do you know when a behavior shows caring?
— What would life be like if no one cared about you? ...if you cared about no one?
— Is it possible to care about people we don't know? Explain.

Communication Counts!
Sending and Receiving Messages

Objectives: The students will:
—define communication and identify ways in which people communicate.
—state rules for effective listening and speaking.
—demonstrate good listening and speaking in a practice session.

Materials: whiteboard

Procedure: Write the word *communication* on the board. Explain to the students that communication is a word that describes the way people send and receive messages. Ask the students to think of ways in which people communicate with each other. (talking face-to-face, phone, writing, computer, television, radio, sign language, body language, etc.)

Ask two volunteers to come to the front of class. Tell them to say something to each other. Point out that during verbal communication between two people, there is always a listener and a speaker. When one person speaks, the other listens. Usually both people take turns in both roles. Tell the students that good communicators know how to listen well, and they also know how to speak well. These are skills that anyone can learn.

Ask the students to help you generate a list of rules for good listening. Suggest that they think of someone who listens well to them, and describe the things that person does. Write their ideas on the board, making sure that the list includes these items:
- Look at the speaker.
- Think about, or picture, what the speaker is saying.
- Don't interrupt.
- Show the speaker that you are listening by nodding, smiling, or making brief comments like, "That's neat" or "Sounds like fun" or "That's too bad." If you don't understand something the speaker says, ask a question.

Now, ask the students to help you generate a list of rules for good speaking. Suggest that they think of someone they know who speaks well and describe what that person does. Write their ideas on the board, making sure that the list includes these items:

• Think about what you want to say before you speak.
• Speak clearly and loud enough to be heard, but don't shout.
• Share the time equally with the other person.
• Don't change the subject unless it's okay with the other person.

List some topics on the board that the students can use during a practice session. For example:
1. A school rule you appreciate and how it helps you.
2. A school rule you don't like, and how you'd change it.
3. The importance of complimenting others, and why it feels good to get a compliment.
4. Other methods of communicating that you use, such as writing and receiving letters or text messages.
5. Your pet and how you train and care for it.

Have the students pair up and sit together. Ask them to decide who is **A** and who is **B**. Announce that the **A**'s will start the first conversation, using the topic of their choice. Tell the **B**'s to join in the conversation, being a good listener at first, and a good speaker every time it is their turn to talk. Review the rules for both listening and speaking.

Allow the partners to talk for 2 to 4 minutes, depending on their level of interest. Then ask the **B**'s to start a new conversation, using a different topic. Review the procedure and the rules as necessary. In a follow-up discussion ask questions to encourage the students to talk about the experience:

Discussion Questions:
— Which rules for good listening were easiest to follow? ... hardest to follow?
— Which rules for good speaking were easiest to follow? ... hardest to follow?
— Which rules, if any, don't you understand?
— How did you feel when you were listening?
— How did you feel when you were speaking.
— How do you feel when someone listens well to you?
— How can being a good listener help you in school? ... in your friendships? ... in your family?
— How can being a good speaker help you?

Hands of Respect

Interview and Art

Objectives: | The studentswill:
— identify respectful actions
—describe an incident in which they demonstrated respect.

Materials: | art paper, scratch paper, and pencils, colored markers, or crayons

Procedure: | Begin by asking the students to think of things that people do to show respect for one another. Focus on small courtesies like greeting a person, saying please and thank you, holding a door, letting someone go first, and shaking hands. Tell the students:

I've heard that some coaches insist that their players shake hands with the members of the opposing team after every game, regardless of whether they win or lose. Why would a coach do that? What message does the coach want to send the other team? What do the players learn by doing this?

After the students have had a few minutes to talk about this display of respect, announce that they are going to participate in an activity about respect, but in this activity instead of shaking hands, they'll draw hands.

Have the students form pairs. Distribute the paper and pencils.

Instruct the students to take turns tracing their patners hand on a sheet of art paper. Point out that the drawing they end up with will not be of their own hand, but of their partner's hand. When they have finished tracing, explain the next step (in your own words):

Interview your partner to find out how your partner shows respect for other people. See if your partner can remember a specific time when he or she said or did something that demonstrated respect for a particular person. Take notes on your scratch paper. Then let your partner interview you. When both of you have finished, use what you've learned to illustrate the tracing of your partner's hand to show the respectful things your partner does. Use letters, symbols, pictures, and other decorations. Your illustration can symbolize lots of respectful actions, or it can tell the story of one particular incident. Decide

who will be the first interviewer and get started.
Make available the art materials. List the following questions on the board to assist the students during their interviews:

Interview Questions:
- How do you show respect for other people?
- Can you remember a specific time when you did something for another person that showed respect? What happened?

When the students have finished their drawings, direct each pair to form a circle with two other pairs. Instruct the students to go around the circle and introduce their partner by showing their hand drawing and describing their partner's respectful actions.

Lead a culminating class discussion.

Discussion Questions:

— A picture of two hands shaking is often used as a symbol of mutual respect and peace. Why do you think that is?
— What are some other ways of showing respect that we included in our drawings?
— If you offered to shake someone's hand and that person refused, what would you think?
— Why is it important to show respect for others?
— What would life be like if no one showed respect for anyone else.

Can You Tell How He or She Feels?
Pantomime and Discussion

Objectives: The students will:
—demonstrate nonverbal behaviors appropriate to specific feelings.
—correctly identify feelings based on body language, facial expressions, and other nonverbal cues.

Materials: descriptions of situations written on small pieces of paper, folded and placed in a container—one description for every two students. The descriptions should portray a variety of emotion-producing situations, like: "You just got a new puppy and your friend is very jealous." or "You and your friend are walking down a dark street at night. Suddenly, you hear a strange noise, but your friend doesn't hear it. He thinks you're making it up."

Procedure: Ask the students to pair up. Have each pair draw one sheet of paper with a situation written on it. Direct each pair to go off to a private place for five minutes and plan a short pantomime of the situation. Explain that the students are to act only with their faces and bodies. They may neither say words, nor make vocal noises. The object is to do such a good job of acting that the class will be able to tell how each actor is feeling in his or her role. If the class can guess the situation, that's fine, but it is not necessary.

When the students have finished planning, have them enact their pantomimes one pair at a time. Enjoy each pantomime and applaud when it is over.

After each pantomime, ask the class to tell the actors how they appeared to be feeling in their roles. Finally, ask the actors to describe the situation they were acting out.

Discussion Questions:
— Do our bodies and faces have a language of their own?
— How easy, or difficult is it to understand what a person is feeling just by observing body language and facial expressions?
— What did you learn about that language through this activity?

Speaking Out Against Bullying
Brainstorming and Discussion

Objectives: The students will:
—Identify interventions they can make to stop bullying and hurtful behavior.
—Recognize that maintaining a peaceful, respectful school climate is everyone's responsibility.

Materials: one copy of the experience sheet, "Stop Bullying! It's Everyone's Responsibility!," for each student

Procedure: Point out that incidents of bullying and hurtful behavior that happen at school often occur in busy places, like hallways, lunch areas, in front of the school and on playgrounds. Although adults don't usually see these things happen, very often other kids are nearby and do witness the incidents, but don't know what to do.

Ask the students to help you brainstorm things that witnesses can do to stop students from bullying one another. Add the following four ideas if they are not mentioned by the group.

1. Confront the person who is bullying. Say something like, "Leave Sally alone. It's wrong to talk mean to others."
2. If the hurtful person is just showing off, don't give him or her an audience. Walk away.
3. If appropriate and safe, distract the kids involved.
4. Create safety in numbers. If you know that a particular student is often harassed, put down, bullied or treated meanly, make sure that the victim is not alone in places where he or she is vulnerable.
5. Report fights and other violent acts.

Write the following headings on the board:
     Who   **How**

Stress that students should talk to an adult about every incident of bullying or violence that occurs. Under the "Who" heading, list appropriate adults.

Discuss ways of reporting that guard the safety of students, such as writing an anonymous note, going to the office after school when the rest of the kids have gone home, or calling a teacher or counselor at home. List these ideas under "How." Make a distinction between tattling and snitching and reporting an incident. Tattling is about wanting to get someone in trouble. Informing an adult is about wanting to help the victim.

Distribute the experience sheets and go over the directions. Define any words with which the children might not be familiar. After allowing the students time to complete the sheet, ask volunteers to read their top five ideas. Facilitate discussion. Try to honor and implement ideas that seem workable, developing action plans, as needed.

Discussion Questions:

— Why do people bully and say and do hurtful things to one another?
— What would you do if you saw your best friend being hurtful to someone?
— What would you do if you saw a student you didn't know bullying someone?
— When you feel angry at someone, what can you do to avoid being mean or disrespectful?
— How can we have a peaceful school where everyone respects everyone else?

Stop Bullying!
It's Everyone's Responsibility
Experience Sheet

It is up to everyone in the school to stop hurtful, bullying behavior. When you and other students decide that it is time to stand up to kids who try to hurt others, you can really make a difference. When you mobilize and take action, you can help put an end to bullying. Wouldn't you like to have a caring, peaceful school?

What can be done to stop kids from harassing each other? List your ideas here:

_____

_____

_____

_____

_____

What can **YOU** do?

_____

_____

_____

_____

Cross out any ideas that involve violence or retaliation. Don't ever do what you want the other person to stop doing. Besides, violence usually makes things worse.

Go back and look at each of your ideas. Ask yourself, "Will this idea really work?" Cross out any ideas that simply will not work.

Now, pick your five best ideas and number them #1 to #5. Make your very best idea #1. That's the idea you should try first when you see someone being mean to another kid!

A Group I Like Belonging To
A Sharing Circle

Objectives: The students will:
—describe benefits of belonging to a group.
—identify qualities of successful groups.

Introduce the Topic: *Today our topic is, "A Group I Like Belonging To." One of the most important things in life for most of us is being part of a group of people whom we enjoy and with whom we share common interests or goals. So today we are going to talk about groups we belong to and how it feels to belong.*

If you decide to share, tell about a group you belong to. It could be a club or organization here at school, at church, or somewhere else. Or it could be a group of friends who get together frequently. Tell about one thing the group does that you enjoy, how you contribute to it, what the group contributes to you, and how you feel about belonging. Today's topic is, "A Group I Like Belonging To."

Discussion Questions: — Why do people join groups, clubs, or organizations?
— What things did we most like about the groups we described?
— What are some of the problems that groups often have?

We Worked Together to Get It Done
A Sharing Circle

Objectives:

The students will:
—describe the importance of cooperation in accomplishing a task.
—state some of the benefits of working with others.

Introduce the Topic:

Our topic for today is, "We Worked Together to Get It Done." Many times we do things all by ourselves, but sometimes it is necessary or more fun to do things with other people. Think of a time when you did something with others. Perhaps you and a friend, or you and your family, worked together to finish something — like a Halloween costume, or a holiday dinner. Maybe you and your Mom did the dishes together, or you and a friend put together a puzzle. Have you and a brother or sister ever worked together to make cookies, or build a sand castle? Think about it for a minute or two, and when you are ready to share, please raise your hand. The topic is, "We Worked Together to Get It Done."

Discussion Questions:

— Do you think it is easier to get the job done with other people helping?
— How did you decide who was going to do what?
— If you were going to do the same job again, would you do the part of the job that you did this time, or would you do a different part of the job? Which part?

A Time I Showed Someone That I Cared

A Sharing Circle

Objectives:

The students will:
—recall incidents in which they showed caring, empathic behavior.
—acknowledge, validate, and support the caring behaviors of others.

Introduce the Topic:

Our topic today is, "A Time I Showed Someone That I Cared." We are all affected by people who care about us. And we have the ability to influence how others feel as well. Think of a time when you showed someone that you empathized and cared and it made the person feel good. Have you ever tried to cheer up a friend who was feeling badly? Perhaps you helped a younger brother with his homework or a little sister tie her shoes. Maybe when your parent was tired from working all day, you helped prepare dinner. Or maybe you told a friend that you understood how he or she felt because you'd felt that same way. How did the person react to your empathy and caring behavior? How did you feel about what you did? Think of the many times you have shown someone that you cared, and share one example with us. Our topic is, "A Time I Showed Someone That I Cared."

Discussion Questions:

— How do we affect the world we live in when we show people that we understand and care about them?
— Why is it important for us to see ourselves as caring people?
— How do we learn to be caring people? How do we learn empathy?

I Helped Someone Who Needed and Wanted My Help
A Sharing Circle

Objectives: The students will describe situations in which they provided assistance to others.

Introduce the Topic: *The topic for this session is, "I Helped Someone Who Needed and Wanted My Help." Can you think of a time when you helped someone do something? Perhaps the person you helped was struggling to carry some things and you offered to take part of the load. Maybe you helped someone work on a project or a math problem that he didn't understand. Or maybe you helped someone finish a job so that the she could go somewhere, and, as a result of your assistance, the person was not only able to do the work faster, but better. Take a few moments to think it over. The topic is, "I Helped Someone Who Needed and Wanted My Help."*

Involve the students. Invite them to take turns speaking. Listen carefully, thank each student who shares, and don't allow negative interruptions. Remember to take a turn yourself.

Discussion Questions:
— What similarities were there in the things we shared?
— How did you know the person you helped wanted your help?
— How did you feel knowing you helped someone who needed help?

I Wanted to Be Part of a Group, But Was Left Out

A Sharing Circle

Objectives:

The students will:
—understand and express the need to belong.
—describe an incident in which they were excluded.
—explain how the need to belong can influence individual behavior.

Introduce the Topic:

One of the most important things to most young people is fitting in — belonging to a group. Although this need continues into adulthood, it is particularly strong among young people, because this is the time when the skills of group membership are learned. Today, we're going to look at what happens when we are refused membership in a group for some reason. We're going to talk about the feelings we experience when we are excluded. Our topic is, "I Wanted to Be Part of a Group, But Was Left Out."

Think back to a time when you really wanted to do something with a group of friends or an organization, but you weren't invited. How did you feel? What did you do? Maybe you tried out for a part in a play or a musical group and didn't make it. How long did it take you to get over it? Have you ever heard some friends talking about something fun they did over the weekend and felt hurt because you weren't asked to join them? Have you ever tried to join in a conversation and been completely ignored? Have you ever felt that you were excluded because you were poorer than the other members of the group, or of a different race, or had a disability? Think about it for a few moments. If you decide to share, describe the situation and tell us how you handled your feelings. Our topic is, "I Wanted to Be Part of a Group, But Was Left Out."

Discussion Questions:

— What did you feel like doing when you were left out? What *did* you do?
— How long did it take you to get over your hurt feelings?
— If a group rejects you because you refuse to conform to its code of behavior, what's the best thing to do?
— What advice would you give a friend who seemed willing to do almost anything to fit in with a group?
— How do attitudes of exclusion hurt us?
— What can you do to develop an attitude of inclusion?

We Used Teamwork to Get It Done
A Sharing Circle

Objectives:

The students will:
—describe a real situation in which a goal was attained through teamwork.
—identify characteristics of a functioning team.
—describe the effects of teamwork on individual commitment and motivation.

Introduce the Topic:

Today, we're going to talk about teamwork and what it can accomplish. Our topic is, "We Used Teamwork to Get It Done."

Think of a situation in which you worked with a team of people to accomplish a goal. You can share something about a team activity in which you've participated here in class, or some other team experience you've had recently. Perhaps you belong to an athletic or debate team that won a competition. Maybe your family worked as a team to clean up the house or hold a yard sale. Or you and some friends may have done something together, like cook a meal, plan a party, or hold a car wash. Tell us what the team was trying to accomplish and how you felt being part of it. Take a few moments to think about it. The topic is, "We Used Teamwork to Get It Done."

Discussion Questions:

— How did most of us feel about being part of a team?
— What makes a team work well together?
— How does the saying, "The whole is more than the sum of its parts," apply to teams?
— How does working with a team on a school assignment affect the quality of your work?
— How does it affect your motivation?
— How would you characterize the differences between a group and a team?

Additional Sharing Circle Topics

A Time When I Accepted Someone Else's Feelings

Someone Didn't Say a Word, But I Knew How S/he Felt

I Didn't Say a Word, But They Knew How I Felt

A Time I Put Myself in Someone Else's Shoes

A Time I Felt Sorry for Someone Who Was Put Down

I Helped Someone Who Needed and Wanted My Help

A Time I Listened Well to Someone

Someone Who Always Understands Me

A Person I Can Share My Feelings With

How I Show That I Care

A Time I Could Have Shown That I Cared, But Didn't

A Time I Failed to Listen to Someone

A Time Someone Really Listened to Me

A Time Someone Failed to Listen to Me

One of the Most Caring People I Know

A Time Someone Understood My Point of View

A Time My Point of View Was Misunderstood

Relationship Skills

Celebrating Our Differences
Class Discussion

Objectives: The students will:
— identify ways in which people are different.
— identify differences between themselves and another student.
— describe benefits and problems that result from differences among people.

Materials: whiteboard, or chart paper and magic marker

Procedure: Discuss with the class the many ways in which people are different. On the board or chart paper, write these terms: race, religion, gender, handicap, ethnicity, economic level, place of residence, education, values.

Define the terms, giving several examples of each. Point out that these are some of the major ways in which people are different. Ask the students:
— How do people react to these differences in others?
— What would the world be like if we were all the same?
— How do you feel when you are with someone who is different from you?
— If you feel uncomfortable around someone who is different from you, what can you do about it?
— How do you feel when someone puts you down because you are different?

Have the students pair up with the person next to them. Tell them to turn toward each other. Say: *Look at your partner. Notice as many things as you can about your partner that are different from you. Tell your partner one of the things you notice. Listen while she or he tells you how you are different. Then think about the ways in which you and your partner are the same, and take turns describing to your partner one of those similarities.*

Discussion Questions:
— How many things did you notice about your partner that were different? ...the same?
— Do you normally notice those things? Why or why not?
— What can you learn from people who are different from you?

Making and Keeping Friends
Role Playing and Discussion

Objectives: The students will:
—describe how all persons need to belong and be accepted by others.
—demonstrate desirable skills for interacting with and relating to others.
—demonstrate tolerance and flexibility in group situations.
—demonstrate respect and understanding of differences among people's cultures, life styles, attitudes, and abilities.

Materials: whiteboard

Procedure: In your own words say to the students: *We all need to be treated in friendly ways. And one of the best ways to be treated well ourselves is to be a good friend to others and to treat them well. So let's talk about friendship today. Let's act out, and show one another, how friendship really works. To get started, let's make a list of some ways to make a friend—ways that work well. Then we'll make a list of ways to keep a friend.*

On the board write the headings "Making Friends" and "Keeping Friends". Under the heading, "Making Friends," list at least three strategies that the students describe. Do the same under the heading, "Keeping Friends." As each strategy is mentioned, discuss how ineffective it would be to do the opposite. For example, if a student says that to make a friend you need to introduce yourself and ask what the person's name is, you might say: *Right. Who wants to be friends with someone who calls you, "What's-your-name?*

Have the students demonstrate the strategies listed. Suggest to the students: *I've got some ideas for situations we can act out using the strategies on our lists. When I describe a situation, if you have an idea which strategy will work, raise your hand. If I call on you, come up in front of the class and act it out. If you want some other actors to help, you may call on them. Let me go first to show you what I mean. The first situation is: You are at a friend's birthday party. One of your friend's cousins, who is your age, is there too—but you've never seen him before. How do you make friends with the cousin?*

Ask volunteers to play the friend who is having the birthday, two or three children at the party (who are having a good time), and your friend's cousin. Tell the volunteers what you would like them to say and do. Then, dramatize the scene, introducing yourself to the cousin and demonstrating friendly behavior toward him or her. For example, you might offer to share the last piece of pizza with him, or pour her some punch when you refill your own glass. Afterward, ask the students: *What do you think of what I did to make friends with this person? How did he or she seem to like what I did?*

Choose volunteers to dramatize several additional scenarios. Help each one select a strategy and choose the appropriate number of actors. Assist with planning, as necessary. When the dramatizations have been completed conduct a discussion with the entire group using these and your own questions.

Discussion Questions:

— What qualities make a good friend?
— Why are friendships important?
— What have you learned from these dramatizations that you can use when you want to make a new friend?
— How can you show a friend that you appreciate what he or she has done for you?

Possible scenarios for the "Making Friends" dramatizations:

1. You are playing a game with some of your friends in your front yard. A new girl in the neighborhood walks up and stands nearby watching.
2. The teacher asks you and a boy in your class whom you don't know very well to take a box of books to the library. You believe this boy is much smarter than you are.
3. A family of a different race moves into a house on your street. The family includes two children about your age. One day the children come out of the house just as you walk by on your way to school.

Possible scenarios for the "Keeping Friends" dramatizations:

1. Your friend telephones you, but you just sat down to dinner with your family and it isn't a good time to talk.
2. Your friend had a fight with her big sister and is feeling terrible.
3. You are at the movies with a friend. Just before the movie starts, another friend comes over and sits beside you and says, "Hi." These two friends of yours don't know each other.

Building Friendship Through Trust
Story and Dramatization

Objectives: The students will:
—act out a fable in which trust is built by caring actions.
—demonstrate that trust is an important element in building friendship.

Materials: the fable *Androcles and the Lion, either in book form or from the internet*; "found" materials to use as props (optional)

Procedure: Read (or tell) the story of Androcles and the Lion. It is an Aesop fable in which Androcles, a runaway slave in ancient Rome, encounters a lion with a large thorn stuck in its paw. He gently pulls the thorn out, much to the relief of the lion. Soldiers capture Androcles and send him back to Rome to stand trial. Another group of soldiers catches the lion and carries him back to Rome also. In those days runaway slaves were punished by being put into a large arena with hungry lions that attacked and ate them. Androcles is sent into the arena at the same time as a hungry lion. However, the lion doesn't attack him; it is the same lion he helped. Androcles and the lion are set free. Androcles is saved because of the trust he built with the lion through his caring actions.

After reading the story, review with the class the sequence of events. List the characters on the board: Androcles, the lion, the cruel master, the soldiers, judges, and crowd at the arena. Discuss what actions each character takes in the story. Announce that the students are going to have a chance to act out the story. Ask volunteers to "become" the characters and guide them through a dramatization of *Androcles and the Lion*. Push back the desks, and use props from around the room. Enact the story several times so that every child has an opportunity to participate in at least one interpretation.

Lead a discussion. When everyone has had an opportunity to act in one dramatization, gather the students together and ask these and other open-ended questions to summarize the story's main concepts:

Discussion Questions:

— How was trust built between Androcles and the Lion?
— What are some caring things that people can do to build trusting relationships?
— Why is it important for friends to trust each other?
— Can you remember a caring action that someone took to win your trust?
— Have you ever taken a caring action to win someone's trust?

Everybody's Got a Point of View
Listening, Writing, and Discussion

Objectives: The students will:
—identify perception as a key element in conflict situations.
—describe how the perceptions of people can differ.
—describe ways of resolving conflict.

Materials: a copy of "The Maligned Wolf" (provided)

Procedure: Call the class together and tell the students that you have a story to read to them, called "The Maligned Wolf."

Begin reading the story. Very quickly, the students will recognize the story as Little Red Riding Hood, told from the point of view of the wolf. Expect excitement and keen interest at this point.

After you have finished reading the story lead a discussion by asking these and your own questions.

Discussion Questions:
— Have you heard this story before? What was different about this version?
— Had you ever thought about how the wolf felt, or considered his point of view?
— Why does everyone have a right to his or her own point of view?
— What does hearing this story in this new way teach us?
— What does this story teach us about conflicts?

Conclude the activity by pointing out that the next time the children are about to get into a conflict with someone, they can help prevent or manage the conflict by considering things from the point of view of the other person and trying to get the other person to consider things from their point of view.

Extension: Have the students write a story that can be retold from the point of view of the villian. Some options are: The Three Little Pigs, Jack and the Beanstalk, Hansel and Gretel.

The Maligned Wolf

By Leif Fearn

The forest was my home. I lived there and I cared about it. I tried to keep it neat and clean.

Then one sunny day, while I was cleaning up some garbage a camper had left behind, I heard footsteps. I leaped behind a tree and saw a rather plain little girl coming down the trail carrying a basket. I was suspicious of this little girl right away because she was dressed funny—all in red, and her head covered up so it seemed like she didn't want people to know who she was. Naturally, I stopped to check her out. I asked who she was, where she was going, where she had come from, and all that.

She gave me a song and dance about going to her grandmother's house with a basket of lunch. She appeared to be a basically honest person, but she was in my forest and she certainly looked suspicious with that strange getup of hers. So I decided to teach her just how serious it is to prance through the forest unannounced and dressed funny.

I let her go on her way, but I ran ahead to her grandmother's house. When I saw that nice old woman, I explained my problem and she agreed that her granddaughter needed to learn a lesson, all right. The old woman agreed to stay out of sight until I called her. Actually, she hid under the bed.

When the girl arrived, I invited her into the bedroom where I was in the bed, dressed like the grandmother. The girl came in all rosy-cheeked and said something nasty about my big ears. I've been insulted before so I made the best of it by suggesting that my big ears would help me to hear better. Now, what I meant was that I liked her and wanted to pay close attention to what she was saying. But she makes another insulting crack about my bulging eyes. Now you can see how I was beginning to feel about this girl who put on such a nice front, but was apparently a very nasty person. Still, I've made it a policy to try to ignore put-downs, so I told her that my big eyes helped me to see her better.

Her next insult really got to me. I've got this problem with having big teeth. And that little girl made an insulting crack about them. I know that I should have had better control, but I leaped up from that bed and growled that my teeth would help me to eat her better.

Now let's face it—no wolf has ever eaten a little girl—everyone knows that. But that crazy girl started running around the house screaming with me chasing her trying to calm her down. I'd taken off the grandmother clothes, but that only seemed to make things worse.

All of a sudden the door came crashing open and a big lumberjack was standing here with his axe. I looked at him and all of a sudden it became clear that I was in deep trouble. There was an open window behind me and out I went.

I'd like to say that was the end of it. But that grandmother character never did tell my side of the story. Before long the word got around that I was a terrible, mean guy. Everybody started shooting at me. I don't know about that little girl with the funny red outfit, but I didn't live happily ever after. In fact, now us wolves are an endangered specie. And I'm sure that little girl's story has had a lot to do with it!

Learning About Each Other
Team Talk

Objectives: The students will:
—recognize and describe their own worth and worthiness.
—identify strengths, talents, and special abilities in self and others.
—practice methods of positive self-talk.
—describe similarities and differences among classmates.

Materials: selected topics (provided on the next page) listed on the board

Procedure: Have the students form teams of two and sit facing each other. Announce that the team members are going to take turns talking to each other about a series of topics. In your own words, explain: *Each person will have two minutes to speak to the topic while the other person listens. The person talking should try to be as open and clear as he or she can be. The person listening should be as good a listener as possible, focusing on the speaker rather than paying attention to other things in the room or to personal thoughts. The listener must not interrupt the speaker for any reason while he or she is talking.*

Select several topics that are appropriate for the age range of your class, and write them on the board. Begin the sequence with the first topic and call time after 1 or 2 minutes (depending on the age of your students). Have the students switch roles and address the same topic again. Follow the same procedure for the remaining topics.

When all the topics have been discussed, ask the teams to stand up and join another pair of students, forming groups of four. Direct each person in the group to introduce his or her partner to the new pair by telling them something about the partner that they just learned. Allow time for one complete round of introductions, then break the groups of four into the original teams of 2 and direct them to join a different pair and introduce each other again, this time using a new piece of information. Repeat this process once or twice more so that the students have the opportunity to introduce their partners several times, while interacting with a number of other students in the class.

Have the students return to their seats and lead a brief discussion.

Discussion Questions:

— What have you learned from this activity about how we are the same? ...about how we are different?
— How does talking with and listening to others help you know them better?
— Do you think that knowing another person well makes you less likely to have negative or bad feelings about that person? Why?
— If you had a problem or conflict with someone, what could be gained by talking and listening to each other?

Topics:

One of my favorite T.V. shows is...

A time I felt afraid

One thing I value in a friend

A way I have fun is...

A game I enjoy playing

Something fun I did on summer vacation

I like it when somebody says to me...

Something I can do for myself is...

I get angry when...

I like people who...

Something I am learning right now

Something I do well is...

If I could have one wish it would be...

Something I really want to do

Something that makes me happy

Something that makes me sad

One thing that makes me a good friend is...

Developing Listening Skills
Demonstration and Small-Group Practice

Objectives: Students will:
— learn and practice a process for active listening.
— explain why effective listening is important in human interactions

Materials: one copy of the experience sheet, "Active Listening" for each student; whiteboard and; several topics written on the board prior to the activity (see suggestions at end of activity)

Procedure: Tell the students that they are going to practice one of the most important communication skills they will ever learn — Active Listening. Write the term on the board, underline the word Active, and ask the students how they think active listening differs from the kind of listening they do all day long, every day.

Accept all ideas and begin to facilitate a discussion about the importance of listening. You might ask the students how they feel when someone really listens to them, and what it feels like to be interrupted or to realize that the other person didn't hear a word they said. In the course of your discussion, make the following points about listening:
- Good listeners are rare.
- In most conversations, people are more concerned with what they want to say than what the other person is saying.
- Good listening requires focus, concentration, and energy.
- To really listen, you have to keep an open mind and heart.
- Listening all by itself is the most effective way to help another person solve a problem or make a decision.

Distribute the "Active Listening" experience sheets. Go over the steps to active listening.

Four Steps to Active Listening
1. Look at the person who is talking.
2. Listen carefully without interrupting, and try to understand what the speaker is saying.
3. Notice the feelings that go with the words.
4. Say something to show that you have been listening.

Discuss specific behaviors involved in each step. For example, point out that listening to the words requires thinking about and understanding their meaning from the speaker's point of view. Noticing feelings involves paying attention to the speaker's tone of voice, facial expression, and posture, and empathizing — imagining what it would be like to be in the speaker's shoes. Saying something back not only proves that you are listening, it helps the speaker clarify his/her thoughts and allows you to check to make sure you are "getting the message."

Demonstrate with a volunteer. Ask a child to join you in the front of the room and to talk for a couple of minutes about something that is important to him/her. Instruct the students to watch carefully and notice what you do. Allow the demonstration to continue long enough for you to give four or five active listening responses. Then thank the volunteer and ask the observers to describe what they saw. Clarify the process and answer questions.

Have the students form groups of six. Ask each group to choose a topic from the board. In your own words, give the groups these instructions:

One person at a time will speak to the topic for 1 minute. When it is your turn, before you speak, you must give an active listening response (restate or paraphrase) what the person before you said. Look at the person when you do this. If you are the first person to speak, you will restate the contribution of the last person.

Time the 1-minute intervals and signal when it is time to switch. (The clear but unobtrusive tone of a chime or bell works well for this purpose.) After every student has had a turn to speak, signal the students to stop. Briefly ask each group how it went, clarifying further, as needed. Then, if time allows, have the groups choose a second topic and repeat the procedure. Conclude the activity with a summary discussion.

Discussion Questions:

— What was the easiest thing about active listening.
— What was most difficult?
— How did it feel to be listened to?
— Why do people so seldom stop and really listen to each other?
— How do you think active listening helps people solve problems?
— How do you think active listening can help people understand each other and get along?

Topics

- What I'd like to do this weekend
- A skill I'm trying to improve
- Something I'm worried about
- My hardest subject in school
- The best time I ever had with a friend

Active Listening
Experience Sheet

What is Active Listening? It's when you listen very carefully and try to understand the ideas and feelings of another person from his or her point of view.

Four Steps to Active Listening

1. Look at the person who is talking.
2. Listen carefully without interrupting, and try to understand what the speaker is saying.
3. Notice the feelings that go with the words.
4. Say something to show that you have been listening.

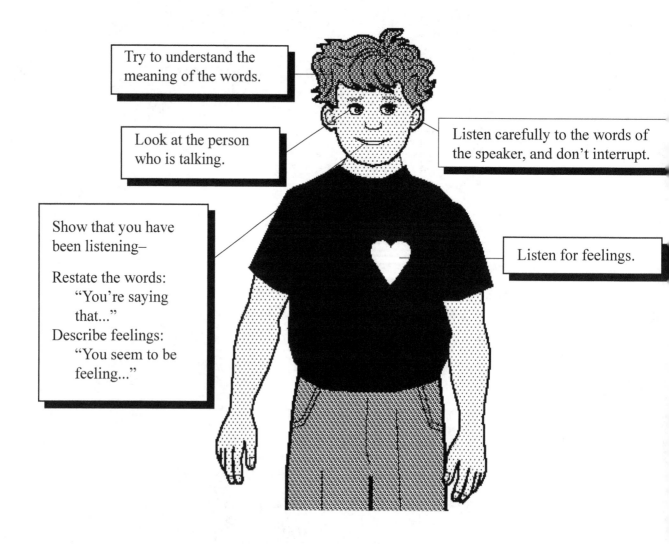

Try to understand the meaning of the words.

Look at the person who is talking.

Listen carefully to the words of the speaker, and don't interrupt.

Show that you have been listening–

Restate the words:
"You're saying that..."
Describe feelings:
"You seem to be feeling..."

Listen for feelings.

Perceptions
Experience Sheet and Discussion

Objectives: Students will:
—demonstrate how different perceptions often lead to conflict.
—discuss ways of resolving conflicts caused by opposing views.

Materials: one copy of the experience sheet, "How Do You See It?" for each student; whiteboard or chart paper and markers

Procedure: Write the word perception on the board, and ask the students to explain its meaning. Definitions might include:
• a mental image or picture
• a unique way of seeing and interpreting something, based on past experiences

Point out that when two people see the same situation very differently — which happens often — the result can be conflict.

Distribute the experience sheets and go over the directions.
Give the students a few minutes to complete the cartoons. Have them share their completed cartoons in groups of four or five. Conclude the activity with a total-group discussion.

Discussion Questions:
— What are people likely to do when their perceptions clash?
— Is there always one right way of seeing something, and does that way make all other perceptions wrong? Explain.
— What kinds of things might cause several of us to see the same incident quite differently?
— What can you do to help two people resolve conflicting views?

How Do You See It?
Student Experience Sheet

Conflicts are often caused by differences in perception. Examine the following cartoons. Draw in the next frame for each cartoon, showing how differences in perception can lead to conflict.

Create a cartoon from your own experiences showing how conflict can arise from differences in perception.

Resolving Conflicts Fairly
Problem Solving and Role Play

Objectives: | The students will:
—consider alternatives in problem-solving situations;
—cultivate skills required to resolve conflicts fairly.

Materials: | whiteboard and writing implements; puppets (optional)

Procedure: | Prior to leading this activity, write down any conflicts observed in the classroom or on the playground. These conflicts may involve either your students or students from other classes.

Call a class meeting, and explain that you want to discuss a problem situation that you have observed. Write these headings across the top of the board: *Reasons, Feelings, Solutions.* Describe one of the conflicts that you observed. Instead of mentioning names, say "Person #1", "Person #2," etc., or use another way to identify the people involved without giving away their identities. Focus the students on the conflict and the moral issues, not on personalities.

Next, challenge the students to think of possible reasons for the problem. Invite them to discuss the reasons while you list them on the board under the first heading (Reasons). Then, ask the children to imagine how each of the parties in the conflict felt. As feeling words are shared, write them on the board under the second heading (Feelings).

Divide the class into groups of three or four and explain that their task is to brainstorm possible solutions to the conflict that are just and fair. Remind the students that seeking the advice of a responsible adult is an acceptable solution. Allow 5 to 10 minutes for brainstorming.

Ask the groups to choose their best solution and share it with the rest of the class. List the solutions on the board under the third heading (Solutions). Be sure to add any alternatives that you believe are important. When all alternatives are listed, discuss the probable consequences of each one. Then invite the students to select the best solution through a show-of-hands vote.

Finally, ask volunteers to role play the conflict, the feelings, and the identified solution. Following the role play, ask the actors and the audience:
— *Would this solution work in real life?*
  ...Why or why not?

If the students indicate that the solution is unworkable, discuss what is needed to make it work. Remind the students that some problems have no easy solutions and more than one alternative may have to be tested. Conclude the activity with a summary discussion

Discussion Questions:

— If you were involved in a similar conflict, how would you try to resolve it? Would your solution be fair to everyone involved?
— Why is it important to think of different alternatives, rather than do the first thing that comes to mind?
— How do you know if an alternative is just or unjust, fair or unfair?
— What can you do if your solution to a problem doesn't work?
— Why is it important to treat others fairly?
— How can we let others know if they are treating us unfairly?
— How can you stand up for yourself without causing a major conflict? What behaviors work best?

Once When Someone Wouldn't Listen to Me
A Sharing Circle

Objectives:

The students will:
—relate an example of failed communication caused by poor listening.
—discuss the importance of listening to good communication.

Introduce the Topic:

Today we are going to talk about one of the frustrations that occurs in the communication process. The topic is, "Once When Someone Wouldn't Listen to Me."

Have you ever tried to get someone to listen to you, and failed? Tell us about it. Maybe you came home wanting to relate an exciting experience to your family and no one would stop long enough to listen. Perhaps you had a question while shopping, but the sales person ignored you. Or maybe you were dealing with a particularly troubling problem and tried to discuss it with a friend, but he or she kept changing the subject or getting distracted. Take a minute to think about it, and tell us about a time when you had an experience like this. The topic is, "Once When Someone Wouldn't Listen to Me."

Discussion Questions:

— What similarities and differences did you notice in our feelings about not being listened to?
— How can you handle situations in which you aren't being listened to?
— What have you learned from this discussion about listening to others?

How I Get People to Pay Attention to Me

A Sharing Circle

Objectives:

The students will:
—explore methods of capturing the attention of others.
—describe feelings generated by attention and lack of attention.

Introduce the Topic:

Today our topic is, "How I Get People to Pay Attention to Me." When you or I want to communicate with someone, first of all we have to get that person to focus on us. There are many ways to do this. For example, if you do something funny, destructive, or bizarre, people will automatically look at you. If you don't want every head in the room to turn, you have to do something less unusual. What do you do?

How do you get the attention of a family member engrossed in a TV program? What do you do to get the attention of a friend some distance from you in a large crowd? How do you capture the attention of someone two tables away in a quiet classroom or library? If you can think of a specific incident in which you used a particular method, tell us about it. The topic is, "How I Get People to Pay Attention to Me."

Discussion Questions:

— When do we need to capture the attention of others?
— What relationship is there between the way you get attention, the kind of attention you get, and how long the attention lasts?
— How do you feel when a person refuses to pay attention to you no matter what you do?
— Why do we need attention from others?

A Friend of Mine Who Is Different From Me

A Sharing Circle

Objectives: The students will:
—identify ways in which friends are unique and different.
—state the importance of respecting differences among people.

Introduce the topic: *Today's topic is, "A Friend of Mine Who Is Different From Me." Think of a friend of yours who is different from you in some important way. Perhaps your friend is of a different race or religion, or is a lot older or younger than you. Maybe your friend would rather read a book while you watch television, or collect aluminum cans while you collect bugs. Do you have a friend who uses a wheelchair, or stutters, or goes to the hospital for dialysis treatments every few days? Don't mention your friend's name, but tell us how he or she is different from you, and what you particularly enjoy about this friendship. Let's think about it for a few moments. The topic is, "A Friend of Mine Who Is Different From Me."*

Discussion Questions:
— When a person thinks or talks differently, or looks different, does that make him or her less worthy of respect? Why or why not?
— What can we gain by having friends who are different from us?
— What would happen if we insisted that all our friends be just like us?

How I Let Others Know I'm Interested In What They Say

A Sharing Circle

Objectives: The students will:
—identify specific behaviors that convey their interest as a listener.
— describe the importance of good listening.

Introduce the Topic: *Our topic for this session is, "How I Let Others Know I'm Interested in What They Say." One way we can let another person know that we are listening and interested in what they have to say is by what we say in response. There are many other things we can do, too. Some of these involve our posture, the way we make eye contact, or whether and how frequently we interrupt them. Think of some of the ways you show other people that you are interested in what they are saying. Also think about how you feel when others listen to you with interest. Select one of the ways that you show interest and tell us about it. Our topic is, "How I Let Others Know I'm Interested In What They Say."*

Discussion Questions:

— How do you think people feel knowing that you are really interested in what they have to say?
— How do you feel knowing that others are interested in what you have to say?
— What can you do to become a more effective listener and communicator?
— Why is good listening so important?

I Got Into a Conflict
A Sharing Circle

Objectives:

The students will:
—describe conflicts they have experienced and what caused them.
—describe ways of dealing with the feelings of others in conflict situations.
—identify strategies for resolving conflicts with peers and adults.

Introduce the Topic:

Our topic today is, "I Got Into a Conflict." Conflicts are very common. They occur because of big and little things that happen in our lives. And sometimes the littlest things that happen can lead to the biggest conflicts. This is your opportunity to talk about a time when you had an argument or fight with someone. Maybe you and a friend argued over something that one of you said that the other didn't like. Or maybe you argued with a brother or sister over what T.V. show to watch, or who should do a particular chore around the house. Have you ever had a fight because someone broke a promise or couldn't keep as secret? If you feel comfortable telling us what happened, we'd like to hear it. Describe what the other person did and said, and what you did and said. Tell us how you felt and how the other person seemed to feel. There's just one thing you shouldn't tell us and that's the name of the other person, okay? Take a few moments to think about it. The topic is, "I Got Into a Conflict."

Discussion Questions:

— How did most of us feel when we were part of a conflict?
— What kinds of things led to the conflicts that we shared?
— How could some of our conflicts have been prevented?
— What conflict management strategies could have been used in the situations that we shared?

When One Person Kept Blaming Another for Causing a Problem

A Sharing Circle

Objectives:

The students will:
—discuss a time when blaming perpetuated a conflict.
—state why blaming is counterproductive to conflict resolution.

Introduce the Topic:

Today in our Sharing Circle, we're going to talk about times when we were part of the "blame game." Our topic is, "When One Person Kept Blaming Another for Causing a Problem."

Blaming is something we are all tempted to do at times. But it usually isn't very helpful. Saying a problem is someone else's fault may get us out of trouble, but it usually doesn't solve the problem. Can you think of a time when you saw one person blame another for just about every part of a problem? Maybe you know someone who gets in trouble a lot and always says it's someone else's fault. Or maybe you have a brother or sister who blames you for just about every problem that comes up at home. Have you heard government leaders who always seem to be blaming each other instead of taking responsibility? Have you tried to settle fights between younger children in which it was hard to figure out what happened because each child blamed the other? Think about it for a few moments. Tell us what happened and how you felt, but don't use any names. The topic is, "When One Person Kept Blaming Another for Causing a Problem."

Discussion Questions:

— Why is blaming not a helpful thing to do?
— How do you feel when someone blames you for something?
— If you're trying to help two people settle a conflict, how can you get them to stop blaming each other?

Additional Sharing Circle Topics

What I Think Good Communication Is

When What Was Said Was Not What Was Meant

A Time When Listening Would Have Kept Me Out of Trouble

I Told Someone How I Was Feeling

A Time I Listened Well to Someone

A Time I Said One Thing But Meant Another

A Time When I Communicated Well

What I Do to Make Myself Understood

A Time When Poor Communication Caused a Misunderstanding

What I Think Poor Communication Is

Something I Did That Helped The Team Succeed

A Time I Felt Included

I Went Out of My Way to Include Someone Else

What I Think Makes a Winning Team

A Time We Cooperated to Get It Done

Responsible
Decision Making

Decisions I Make
Experience Sheet and Discussion

Objectives: | The students will:
—clarify personal beliefs and attitudes and how these affect decision-making.
—describe how decisions affect self and others.

Materials: | one copy of the experience sheet, "Thinking About Decisions," for each student

Procedure: | Distribute the experience sheets. Read the directions to the children while they read along silently. Talk about the different types of decisions and give an example of each.

Have the students complete the experience sheets.

Lead a discussion. Go over the list of decisions on the experience sheet. Ask for a show of hands indicating which of the five categories the students chose for each decision. Discuss the reasons for their choices. Then ask volunteers to tell the group about some of their own decisions described at the bottom of the experience sheet. Facilitate discussion.

Discussion Questions: | — Were most of your decisions automatic?
— Were many decisions out of your control?
— What kinds of decisions do you give a lot of thought?
— Which decisions were affected by your personal beliefs? Your attitudes?
— Which decisions were affected by your friends?
— Which decision were affected by your parents?
— Which decisions were affected by your interests?
— What have you learned about decision making from this activity? What have you learned about yourself?

Thinking About Decisions
Experience Sheet

Everyone makes decisions daily. Some of the decisions are more important than others. Some are so important that they require lots of thought and study before a decision is made. Others are automatic. Here are five categories for showing how decisions are made:

0 = Not under my control
1 = Automatic
2 = Sometimes think about it

3 = Think about it, but don't study it
4 = Study it a little bit
5 = Study it a lot

Below is a list of decisions. In front of each, put the number that stands for how you would make the decision:

____ To get up in the morning
____ To tell the truth
____ What books to read
____ To say please and thank you
____ To stop at STOP signs
____ To ride a bicycle
____ Where to throw trash

____ To criticize a friend behind his/her back
____ What to eat and when
____ To study for a test
____ To use drugs
____ What to do when you grow up
____ To go to school
____ What TV show to watch

Think back over the past week. On the lines below, describe some decisions you have made. Try to include one decision in each of these areas:

• decisions about what to do _____

_____

• decisions about school _____

_____

• common, everyday decisions _____

_____

• health and safety decisions _____

_____

• decisions about what is right and wrong _____

_____

Decisions, Decisions, Decisions!
Presentation and Discussion

Objectives: The students will:
—identify alternatives in decision-making situations.
—clarify personal beliefs and attitudes and state how these affect decision-making.

Materials: chart paper and magic marker or whiteboard

Procedure: Introduce the activity. Say to the students: *We all make many decisions every day. Sometimes decisions are easy to make and sometimes they are hard. When they are hard, it helps to know some steps to take in making them. I'm going to read you a story about a girl who has a tough decision to make. Afterwards, let's see if we can figure out what she ought to do.*

Karen and Susan are friends. They sit next to each other at school. Karen is good at math. Susan doesn't like math, and has trouble with it. Tomorrow, their teacher is going to give the class a big math test. Susan comes up to Karen after school. She looks worried. She asks Karen if she can copy her answers on the test tomorrow. Karen doesn't say anything. But at home that night, she worries. She has to decide what to do.

Give the students a few moments to think about the situation. Then ask them:
—Why is Karen worried?
—What decision does Karen have to make?
—If Karen lets Susan copy her answers, what could happen?
—If Karen says no, what could happen?
—If Karen does nothing at all, what could happen?
—If you were Karen, would you talk to someone before deciding? Who?
—What decision do you think Karen should make?

During the discussion, you and the children will no doubt name most of the steps in the decision-making process. As they are mentioned, write them on the chart paper or board.

1. What is the decision about? (definition)
2. What are my choices? (alternatives)
3. What could happen if I make each choice? (consequences)
4. What is the best decision?

Read through the steps with the students and discuss them. Then present the additional decision-making situations. Ask the students to pretend that they are the person making the decision. Go through all of the steps together and then ask the students what decision they would make and why. Facilitate discussion throughout and at the conclusion of the activity.

Additional Decision-Making Situations

- Rick's uncle is visiting for the weekend. He wants to take Rick out exploring on a big boat. They will be gone all weekend. Rick would have to miss Little League practice. His team is getting ready for the play-offs. He has to make a decision.

- Leah likes Carol better than any baby-sitter she's ever had. Carol plays games with Leah and her little brother. She reads to them and is always nice. But last night, when Leah got up to go to the bathroom, she saw Carol pouring herself a glass of wine from the refrigerator. When Carol saw Leah watching, she seemed upset. She said, "Don't tell anyone, okay?"

- Greg and Paul ask Ruben to ride his bike to the shopping mall with them. They offer to take him to a movie. Ruben really wants to go, but the brakes on his bike aren't working very well. He could probably make it, but he'd have to ride through heavy traffic. He has to decide what to do.

Discussion Questions:

— Why is Rick's decision difficult? (He has to decide between two desirable and important activities.)
— Why is Carol's decision difficult? (She faces a moral dilemma — informing her parents vs. protecting her baby-sitter.)
— Why is Ruben's decision difficult? (He has to decide whether to risk his own safety for a little fun.)
— What feelings would you have in Rick's situation? ...in Carol's? ...in Ruben's?
— How do you feel when you have to make a tough decision? How do you feel after you have made the decision?
— How does doing the right thing, even when it's very tough, make you feel better.

Recognizing Peer Pressure

Brainstorming and Discussion

Objectives: | The students will:
—describe peer pressure as an opportunity to exercise responsibility..
—identify types of peer pressure and their effects.

Materials: | whiteboard or chart paper and magic marker

Procedure: | Write the heading "Peer Pressure" on the board or chart paper. Gather the students together and, in your own words, define the term. For example, say: *A peer is someone who is like you in many ways. Your peers are about the same age as you are, they go to school like you do, and they like many of the same things that you like. The other children in this class are your peers. My peers are other adults who went to college and have jobs. For example, the principal and the other teachers in this school are my peers.*

Pressure is a type of force. For instance, when I push this door open, or close this drawer, I do it with the pressure of my hand (demonstrate). That's a type of physical pressure. The kind of pressure we're going to talk about today, however, is not physical. Instead, it comes from the words and actions of other people. Peer pressure comes from the words and actions of your peers. If someone in this class tries to get you to do something that you don't want to do, that's an example of peer pressure. If your friend tries to get you to do something you might want to do, but aren't sure about, that's peer pressure, too. Sometimes peer pressure is good, and sometimes it's harmful. Peer pressure is good when it makes us consider things that are good for us — like being friendly or playing fair. Peer pressure is harmful when it tries to get us to do something that is wrong or unhealthy.

Write the following (or another) example on the board or chart:

- Billy is supposed to go to the library after school and pick out some books. Ted and Jeff try to convince him to play catch instead.

Discuss the example with the students. Use these and other open-ended questions:
— Is this an example of good peer pressure or harmful peer sure?
— If Billy says no, and the other boys accept his answer, is it peer pressure?
— How do you think Billy feels when his friends try to get him to do something he's not supposed to do?
— What could happen if Billy gives in and plays catch instead of going to the library?
— What could happen if Billy refuses to play with his friends?
— What would you say if you were Billy? What would you do? What might happen if you said or did that?

One at a time, list and discuss other examples of peer pressure. Use some of your own, ask the students to contribute some, or use the examples provided. Discuss each one with the children, asking open-ended questions (like those above) tailored to the example. When the students suggest ways of responding to a harmful pressure situation, write them down on the board/chart. Discuss how well each suggestion would work.

Peer-Pressure Situations:

* Mary wants to copy Angela's answers on a test.
* Dennis tries to get Bruce to get up earlier, so he won't be late for school.
* Molly wants Chris to ride his bike with her to the park on a other side of town, even though his parents told him not to ride that far.
* John wants Jose to smoke a cigarette.
* Judy tries to convince Michael to use hand signals when he rides his bike.
* Kelly urges Maria to wear her mother's pearl necklace without permission.
* Paul tries to convince Tammy that school is boring and she shouldn't study so much.
* Jean and Lita think Janice is weird and urge Diane not to talk to her.
* Diane urges Jean and Lita to invite Janice to play with them.
* Joey tells Manny that boys shouldn't have teddy bears and urges Manny to throw his in the dumpster.

Conclude the activity. Emphasize that peer-pressure situations can take many forms, both good and harmful. It is important to recognize harmful peer pressure situations and know how to handle them.

Making the Right Decision
Discussing Moral Dilemas

Objectives: The students will:
—differentiate right choices from wrong choices.
—identify different methods of evaluating behavior.
—recognize inner conflict over doing the right thing.
—describe times when they did the right thing.

Materials: several 3X5 cards for each student

Procedure: Begin by explaining to the students that this activity is about how decisions are made, and about deciding to do what's right in situations that call for moral judgment. In your own words state:

Every time you take an action of any kind, that action is preceded by a decision. So you are making decisions constantly. Sometimes the decisions seem automatic, like the decision to sit at your desk, or wave to a friend across the room. Other times, the decision requires some thought. Maybe you have different choices, like whether to study or play games on your computer. However, if your mom told you not to play games until your homework was finished, then it would be right to study, and wrong to play games. Many decisions involve choosing between right and wrong behaviors. Sometimes the difference between right and wrong is very clear. Other times it is more difficult to figure out.

Present the following dilemma to the students:

You are in a store with two friends, Chris and Lee, looking at some neat merchandise. Lee disappears down a nearby aisle. After a few minutes, you decide to join Lee. When you turn the corner, you see Lee slip a package into his backpack. You also see a store employee a few yards away who apparently saw the same thing you did. You stop in your tracks and quickly back up, wondering what to do.

Ask the students,

— What are your choices?

List their ideas on the board. Encourage them to see numerous possibilities, including:

- Go back and rejoin Chris, hoping the store employee didn't notice you.
- Go back, grab Chris and head for the door, hoping that Lee will be all right and will join you later.
- Grab Lee and run for the door.
- Walk over and quietly urge Lee to put the package back because someone is watching.
- Urge Lee to put the package back because stealing is wrong.
- Try to distract the employee with a question.
- Stand your ground and wait to see what happens. If the employee confronts Lee, tell the truth about what you saw.
- Wait to see what happens. If the employee intervenes, pretend you don't know Lee.

When the students run out of ideas, go back and discuss the options. Talk about what's right and wrong with each idea, and what might happen as a result of each choice.

Distribute the 3x5 cards. Read aloud one of the remaining situations. Give the students a few minutes to write down on a card a brief description of what they would do. Collect the cards and read each one aloud without divulging the writer's name. Make notes on the board about the various choices mentioned.

Again, engage the students in a discussion about what's right and wrong in the situation, and the possible consequences of various choices.

Follow the same procedure with the other story.

Story 1

On the last day of school, Mark gets his parents' permission to walk home through a large park with his friend Henry, rather than take the school bus. Though Mark promises to stay on the marked hiking trails, Henry talks him into taking a short cut up a remote wooded area to get to their neighborhood. Part way through, the boys are attacked by a swarm of bees. The bees chase and sting them. Henry, who doesn't run as fast as Mark, gets the worst of it. At the first house they come to, they are given shelter and first aid, and the owner calls their parents, police and paramedics. While the paramedics are preparing to take Henry to the hospital, Henry whispers tearfully to Mark not to tell anyone they went off the trail. The police officer wants to know where the attack took place so he can send an exterminator to kill the bees and determine if the hive belonged to dangerous Africanized or killer bees. Mark's parents want reassurance that their son obeyed their orders. Mark is torn. He doesn't think it's fair to kill the bees. If he says he and Henry were on the trail, the exterminator probably won't find the hive and he and Henry won't get into any trouble. But if they don't find the hive, they won't know if the bees are Africanized. He's also worried about Henry, whose father is very strict. If you were Mark, what would you do?

Story 2

Tami plays first clarinet in her school's award-winning band. The band has been raising money for over two years to take a concert tour of schools in Europe. The trip will start during Spring vacation, but continue a week longer, so only those musicians with a B average or better will be allowed to go. Tami is right on the edge. She must get an A on the upcoming Algebra test in order to get a B in math, and without a B in math she will lose out on the trip. Tami's friend Art, also a band member, works out a code that will enable him and two other classmates to signal Tami with the correct answers. He insists that the co-conspirators rehearse the system at his house the night before the test. Tami is a good student and has always done her own work. This scheme doesn't feel right, but she has her heart set on the trip. If you were Tami, what would you do?

Discussion Questions:

— Why is it sometimes hard to make the right decision?
— How often has fear of punishment, or fear of the consequences, caused you to make a wrong decision?
— What determines whether a decision is right or wrong?
— When should you ask for help in making a decision?
— Does it take more courage to do the wrong thing and worry about getting caught, or to do the right thing and accept the consequences?

Who's Responsible?
Stories, Decision Making, and Discussion

Objectives:

The students will:
—practice making decisions about who bears responsibility in specific situations
—describe responsible behaviors.

Procedure:

Begin this activity by announcing to the students that you have one or two stories to read (or tell) them. Two excellent stories are summarized below.

The Bell of Atri

The king installed a bell in a tower in the Italian town of Atri, and announced to the people that the bell should only be rung when someone felt he or she had been wronged. Through the years, every time the bell was rung, the judges came together to right each wrong. After years of wear and tear, the bell's rope became old, torn, and shortened. This worried the judges, because if a child were wronged, the child would not be able to reach the rope. To solve this problem, a man tied a grapevine to the end of the rope, making it long and strong enough for even the smallest child to operate.

In the hills above Atri lived a man who had been a famous knight when he was younger. He had a great horse that was his best friend and had saved him from many dangers in his knighthood days. But as the man grew older, he became a miser and loved nothing but gold. He sold everything he could for money except his horse, which had grown very old and feeble. The man thought no one wanted the horse, so he turned it out without trying to sell it. The poor horse could barely find enough grass to eat and was slowly starving and freezing from the cold. People ran the horse off and treated it badly.

One day, shortly after the grapevine was tied to the rope of the bell of Atri, the horse was looking for food and wandered near the tower. The horse saw the green leaves on the grapevine and took a bite, which pulled the rope. The bell sounded and it seemed to say, "Someone has done me wrong!" The judges came running and immediately saw the situation: The poor horse was telling the world how it felt in the best way it could. They ordered the old miserly knight brought before them, and made him spend half of his gold on food, a new stable, and a green pasture for his poor old horse.

Icarus and Daedalus

Daedalus was a very famous and clever builder and artist in ancient Greece. King Minos of the nearby island of Crete had a big problem: A minotaur (a horrible monster that was half bull, half man) was on the loose. Minos succeeded in getting Daedalus to come to Crete to build a prison that would hold the beast. Icarus, the young son of Daedalus, went with his father. Daedalus designed and built the prison, but when he and his son wanted to sail back to Greece, Minos imprisoned them in the top of a tower. He wanted Daedalus to be on call to take care of any other problems that might arise.

Being very clever and never giving up, Daedalus came up with a method of escape, which he learned from the sea gulls as he watched them fly. After collecting lots of feathers, he created a huge pair of wings fastened together with string and wax. Then he taught himself to use them. Next, Daedalus made a pair for Icarus, and gave his son flying lessons. Then Daedalus and Icarus waited for the perfect day when the winds would be just right for flying back home to Greece.

When the right day came, father and son prepared to leave, but first Daedalus gave Icarus a warning: "Don't fly too low, because the sea spray will get your wings wet and bog them down, or too high, because the sun's rays will melt the wax. Either way you'll crash. Just stay by me and you'll be fine." As they took off, both were scared, but soon they got used to flying and Icarus in particular became full of joy. He forgot his father's warning and sailed higher and higher.

Daedalus yelled for his son to come back, but Icarus was completely overcome with the urge to get as close to the heavens as he could. Little by little the feathers came off, then all of a sudden the wax melted completely and no matter how much he beat his arms up and down Icarus could not stay aloft; he fell into the sea and drowned. Daedalus, the sad father, finally found his son's body and carried it to Greece for burial. Later he built a temple over the grave in memory of the son he loved so much, who failed to follow his guidance at a crucial time.

After reading (or telling) the stories, engage the students in a discussion concerning who was, or should have been, responsible for what. Help the students recognize three moral lessons illustrated in the stories:

- People are obligated to care for each other and their animals.
- Parents are responsible for guiding their children.
- Children have the responsibility to listen to, and follow, their parent's guidance.

Next, read the scenarios to the students, asking the accompanying questions and facilitating discussion.

Scenarios

1. You and your parents are visiting the home of some relatives or friends. One of the boys in the family, who is your age, throws a rock at his little brother. No adults are around at the time.
   —Do you have a responsibility to do anything?
   —If so, what is the most responsible thing to do?

2. You enter a store with one of your parents, and see a wallet on the floor. You pick up the wallet and look inside. You see that the wallet contains money. Your parent has not noticed any of this.
   —Do you have a responsibility to do anything?
   —If so, what is the most responsible thing to do?

3. Your sister begged for a puppy for her birthday and got one. But now it is almost a year later, and she has practically forgotten the dog. She rarely gives him fresh water or feeds or plays with him.
   —What is the most responsible thing to do in this situation?

4. Your friend comes up to you before school starts and tells you she didn't do her homework and wants to copy yours.
   —Who is responsible for your friend's homework?
   —What is the best thing for you to do?

5. Your friend is angry at his sister and his Dad. Yesterday, he got into a fight with his sister, which he says was all her fault, but his Dad punished them both. Today, you are at your friend's house and you are thinking about what happened.
   —Do you have any responsibilities in this situation?

Conclude the activity with more questions and a summary discussion.

Discussion Questions:

— Imagine that you are the little kid having rocks thrown at him in the first scenario, or the person who lost the wallet in the second scenario, or the dog in the third scenario. How would you feel if no one was responsible enough to care about you or help you?
— Is it always a good idea to help someone who is asking for help? Is helping always the most responsible thing to do?
— How can you tell if a situation is your responsibility?
— Why is it important to know who is responsible for what?

Responsibility in Action
Discussion and Experience Sheet

Objectives: The students will:
—relate specific examples of responsible behavior
— monitor and describe responsible and irresponsible behaviors.

Materials: two or more copies of the experience sheet, *Responsibility Log,* for each student; whiteboard

Procedure: Begin by discussing the meaning of the word *responsibility.* List the following components of responsibility on the board and ask the students to think of *specific* examples that might fit under each one. Invite them to share incidents from their own experience.

Accountability
- Think before you act.
- Before you make a decision or take an action, think about how it will affect the other people involved. What will be the consequences?
- When you do something wrong or make a mistake, admit it and accept the consequences. Don't blame others or make excuses.
- Give credit to others for their achievements.
- Do what you should do, or have agreed to do, even if it is difficult.

Excellence
- Set a good example in everything you do.
- Do your best.
- Keep trying — don't quit.
- Make it your goal to always be proud of your performance (schoolwork, homework, projects, completed chores, athletic, or other performances, etc.)

Self-control or self-restraint
- Always control yourself.
- Control your temper — don't throw things, scream, hit others, or use bad language.
- Wait your turn.
- Show courtesy and good manners.

Being a good sport
- Win and lose with grace
- Accept congratulations when you win; accept responsibility when you lose.
- Take pride in how you play the game, not just whether you win.

Continue the discussion until the students understand the meaning of responsibility and many specific examples of responsible behavior have been shared. Then announce that, for the next few days, the students are going to keep logs describing actions that are clearly responsible and clearly not responsible.

Distribute the "Responsibility Log" and go over the directions with the students. Explain that the students should write down actions that they know are responsible (doing their best on a homework assignment and completing it on time; admitting when they forget to do a chore; congratulating the other team when they lose a game, etc.) as well as actions they feel are not responsible (not paying attention in class, blaming another person, procrastinating on an assignment, etc.).

Announce a date when the completed logs are due. Allow from two to five days, depending on the maturity of your students. Commend (for their responsibility) those students who complete the logs on time.

Before collecting the logs, have the students share their results in groups of four. Finally, lead a culminating class discussion.

Discussion Questions:

— Which do you have more of, actions which are responsible or actions which are not responsible?
— What surprised you about the results of your log?
— How do you feel when you take a responsible action? How do you feel when your actions are not responsible?
— In which area of responsibility do you think you need to improve?

Responsibility Log
Experience Sheet

For the next few days, pay close attention to your actions. Write down things you say and do that are clearly responsible actions. Also, write down things you say and do that you realize are not responsible actions.

Action	Responsible? Yes or No	Reactions of Others	I Learned

Values Affect Decisions
Decision Making Dilemas

Objectives: | The students will:
—evaluate their own and others' behaviors,
—discuss how values and ethics are formed
—explain the difference between thinking about and doing something bad.

Materials: | whiteboard; chart paper, marking pens, masking tape, and three signs prepared prior to the session (see "Procedure")

Procedure: | Ask the students if they know what the term ethics means. Write the word on the board, listen to any ideas that the students voice, and clarify that ethics are principles or values having to do with right and wrong.

Ask the students: *Who can tell us about something you've done in the last few days that was a good thing to do?*

Call on volunteers. After each person shares, ask him or her: How did you know that what you did was a good thing to do?

Discuss various ways of knowing: because it feels good, because parents have said it's good, because anything else would feel bad, etc.

Next, ask the students: *Who is willing to tell us about a bad thing you've done recently?*

Again, ask each volunteer: *How do you know that what you did was bad?*

Be sure to take a turn yourself and share something that you're not proud of having done. Emphasize that all people do bad things at times. That doesn't mean that they are bad people, only that they made a mistake. The most important thing is to recognize and admit that you've done something wrong and learn from the experience.

Place these three signs (prepared ahead of time) on the wall:

• I think that was a very good thing to do.
• I'm not sure whether it was good or bad.
• I think that was a very bad thing to do.

Tell the students that you are going to read them some situations. They are to go and stand in front of the sign that matches what they think or feel about the behavior of the principal person in the situation.

One at a time, read the situations from the list on the following page. Give the students time to decide and position themselves. Then walk up to each group and ask individual students, "Why are you standing here?"

Interview the students about their reasons for deciding the way they did. Underscore examples that demonstrate different perceptions of what happened in the situation. When values have played a clear role in someone's decision, discuss with the class how values are developed.

Have the students return to their seats. Conclude the activity with a general discussion.

Discussion Questions:

— What's the difference between having a bad thought or feeling, and actually doing a bad thing?
— When you find yourself thinking about doing something bad, how do you stop yourself from doing it?
— How do we learn the difference between good and bad, right and wrong?
— If you know that a friend is about to do something bad, should you try to stop him or her? Why or why not?
— How about just saying, "It's not my problem" and not worrying about it?

Extension:

Consider spreading the various parts of this activity over two or three days. Then spend more time examining each part: good behaviors; bad behaviors; the role of values and perceptions; the differences between thinking/feeling and doing; and how ethics are developed.

Situations

- Keith beats up a younger boy because he overhears the boy call his sister a bad name.

- Without asking, Maria borrows an old ring of her mother's. When she loses it, Maria decides not to say anything. Chances are her mother won't notice that the ring is missing for a long, long time.

- Willie is in a big hurry to get home. He can't see any cars in either direction so he crosses on the red signal.

- Linda sees a girl she doesn't like cheating on a spelling test, so she tells the teacher.

- Linda sees her friend cheating on a social studies quiz, and doesn't say anything to anyone.

- Sandie overhears the teacher scolding two classmates for leaving a mess on the work table. Sandie helped make the mess, but she doesn't speak up.

- Three tough kids are making fun of a new student. Reginald is a little afraid of the tough kids, but he stands up for the new student anyway, telling the tough kids to get lost.

- Jon stays up very late watching old movies and can barely move the next morning. He decides to stay home from school and get some sleep.

- Roberto finishes his homework early, so he helps his younger brother with his homework.

- Jeanne knows that Mr. Snipes hates to have kids cut across his lawn, but she also knows that Mr. Snipes is on vacation, so she cuts across anyway.

What Would You Do?
Group Work and Discussion

Objectives:	The students will: —determine ethical behaviors for typical self-interest situations —identify the underlying moral values in specific situations.
Materials:	one copy of the experience sheet, *Decision Point!*, for each small group; pencils/pens
Procedure:	Introduce the concepts of *self-interest* and *self-protection*. Point out that most of us know the difference between right and wrong. We often know exactly what we *should* do in a situation, even though we don't always do it. When we desire something for ourselves, we often let that desire get into a fight with our knowledge about what is right and wrong. Sometimes self-interest wins.

Have the students form groups of four or five. Give each group a copy of the experience sheet and go over the directions. In your own words, elaborate: *Take turns reading the situations aloud in your group. After a situation is read, brainstorm ideas about what the person in the situation should do. Have a recorder write down all the ideas. When the group runs out of ideas, go around the circle and take turns saying what you as an individual would do if you were in that situation.*

In a follow-up discussion, focus on the moral values underlying each situation. Emphasize that when these moral values get into contests with self-interest, the moral values should always be the winners. Do not equivocate on this point.

Discussion Questions:	— Which moral value are you breaking when you steal? (Honesty) — What moral values are you breaking if you treat someone badly just because he or she is different? (Respect/Kindness) — What moral values are you breaking when you keep something that doesn't belong to you? (Honesty/Responsibility) — What moral value are you breaking if you blame someone else (or allow someone to get blamed) for something you did? (Honesty/Responsibility/Respect) — Why are decisions like these sometimes hard to make? — How does making the right decisions help you become a good person?

Decision Point!
Experience Sheet

Take one situation at a time. Read it aloud and talk about it with your group. Make a list of the things you think the person in the situation should do. Then go around the group and take turns answering the question, "What would *you* do?"

1. Norman likes many toys, especially cars. At the toy store, he sees a car he has wanted for a long time, but it costs too much money. He looks around and sees that no one is watching. He could easily slip the car into his pocket. *What should Norman do?*

2. Lisa comes out to lunch late and sees her friends making fun of a new girl. Lisa likes the new girl and thinks that her friends should not make fun of her just because she is new. She wants to be with her friends because she likes them, but doesn't like to be mean. *What should Lisa do?*

3. Trahn finds a wallet on the ground. Inside is a twenty dollar bill — just enough money to buy his mother something nice for her birthday. Trahn knows he should return the wallet, but he wants to surprise his mom. *What should Trahn do?*

4. Shelly cracks the glass on her mother's computer monitor. She cracks it with her little sister's bat, which she isn't supposed to be using in the house. If she gets in trouble she won't be able to go to her friend's birthday party. She could easily blame it on her sister. *What should Shelly do?*

5. Eric's mom made a tray of fresh brownies. Those are Eric's favorite. His mom says that Eric can have only two. When Eric finishes his two brownies, he sees the plate sitting on the counter by itself and his mom isn't around. Eric really wants more brownies. *What should Eric do?*

6. Rosa and her best friend get in a fight. Rosa really wants to make up, but her friend won't talk to her. Rosa knows that she did something mean and wants to apologize, but her friend did something mean, too. *What should Rosa do?*

Sweet Revenge
Story and Discussion

Objectives:	The students will: —identify the moral values operating in a complex interpersonal situation — recognize how values guide actions.
Materials:	one copy of Sweet Revenge The Story for each student (optional)
Procedure:	You may read the story to the students, have them take turns reading, or distribute copies of the story and allow each student to read independently. Ask the discussion questions, encourage discussion by helping the students to identify the values inherent in the story, evaluate the motives and actions of the characters, and consider alternative courses of actions.
Discussion Questions:	— What moral values played a part in this story? — Did Mr. Brickle show respect for the children who walked by his house? Did he show caring? — Did the children show respect for Mr. Brickle? How did they feel about him? — Was it right or wrong of Mr. Brickle to take James' bike? — Why did James' parents make him apologize to Mr. Brickle? — Was it right or wrong of the boys to plot to get even with Mr. Brickle? — How could the boys have handled their anger toward Mr. Brickle? — What do you think of the other boys for promising to stand by James and then running away instead? — Did James fake the other boys out? Did he guess that they would run away? — How would you have felt if you were James? What would you have done?

Sweet Revenge the Story

by Thomas Pettepiece

"I dare you," Morey said.

James gulped. Morey had dared him before to do things at school, like ten pull-ups on the high bar, or hijack someone's ball during recess. Once he even dared him to stick out his tongue at the teacher while she wasn't looking, which he did, though he could have sworn she saw him at the last minute when she turned her head and his tongue retreated quickly into hiding.

Never had he felt such conflict. His stomach gurgled like an empty cavern. Beneath him he felt wobbly rubber legs, just like he saw on the Saturday morning cartoon characters. Morey, James, and three other boys were standing right below Mr. Brickle's big picture window, where Mr. Brickle stood every day after school and watched the children walk home. If he saw anyone goofing off, or bothering someone, or worst of all, stepping on his property in the slightest — on any part — the grass or the flower bed with chrysanthemum bulbs waiting for Spring, he would pound on the window and shake his fist at them. And if that didn't work, he would disappear from view for a moment, then reappear on the porch shouting, "You kids better stay out of the yard if you know what's good for you." No one ever really knew what would not be good for them if they didn't, but no one ever had the courage to defy the old man and find out. Until now that is.

All eyes were on James. The growing silence was starting to sound like cowardice in the face of pressure. "Come on James. Are you or aren't you?"

"Yeah. You're the one who's always talking so tough, saying 'Mr. Brickle is as dumb as a pickle,' and stuff like that. Are you going to throw that rock or not?"

James had wanted to for a long time, ever since Brickle had singled him out for parking his bike on the sidewalk in front of Brickle's house. James's dog had gotten loose, and James stopped his bike there so he could chase the mongrel on foot. When he came back the bike was gone. James didn't get it back for a week — not until he went over and apologized to Mr. Brickle, even though his parents said James didn't do anything wrong. The sidewalk was public property, they said. Still, Mr. Brickle or someone else could have tripped trying to go around the bike blocking the walkway.

That night after dinner, James and his buddies had met on the corner of Mr. Brickle's street and decided to get even with the old man by breaking his precious picture window. Then he couldn't stand there and stare at them anymore. Tonight was the perfect time, since, on their way home from school, they'd seen Mr. Brickle's son drive off with him. It was twilight, dark enough so the boys could not be seen crouching in the bushes beneath the window, but light enough that they were able to find the medium-size rock James now held in his hand.

"You're chicken, James," one of them said.

"All talk and no action," said another.

"You've got a yellow streak down your back longer than the highway," Morey blurted out.

"Well, you do it then, Big Mouth," James shot back.

"He didn't take my bike, man."

"Yeah, but he's yelled at you as much as me, calling you a punk kid and a juvenile delinquent."

The other boys murmured. It was true. Brickle had insulted them all at one time or another, and not one kid who walked by his house had been spared the wrath of his cruel words. Hadn't Mr. Brickle ever been a kid? What was wrong with him anyway?

"Well, James?" they all echoed in unison. "It's getting dark. Let's go. Now or never."

"Okay, okay. On one condition."

"What?" asked Morey.

""That we're all in this together. If anyone gets caught, we all get caught. And if anyone squeals, the rest will pound him. Got it?"

They all looked at each other for a moment, then back at James.

"Okay. Do it."

James stepped back so he could see the entire front of the house. It was an old wooden house, built over sixty years ago, with brick around the bottom. The section with the big window jutted out toward the street, so while it provided a perfect viewing stand for Mr. Brickle, it also made a perfect target.

James tossed the rock up and down in his palm, higher each time. He eyed the glass as though it were a bullseye on a shooting range. "Let's get Brickle, let's get Brickle," he began to chant. His arm was up in the air now, making circles as if he were preparing to throw the rock all the way to China. "Let's get Brickle," the other boys chanted with him. "Get Brickle, get Brickle, get Brickle," the rhythm continued as the boys spread out so they wouldn't get hit by huge chunks of glass from the enormous window.

"One, two..." James shouted.

"RUN!" cried Morey as they all scattered like squirrels fleeing a hunter.

"Three!"

But James held onto the rock, and then he just let it drop harmlessly to the ground. He turned away just in time to see the other boys disappear around a corner. James had made his decision.

When I Got to Share in Making a Decision

A Sharing Circle

Objectives:

The students will:
—describe decision-making processes in which they have participated.
—explain how participating in the process affects their commitment to a decision.

Introduce the Topic:

Today's topic is, "When I Got to Share in Making a Decision." We all like to be part of the decision-making process. We want to help our families plan vacations and decide what movies to see. We want to be involved when our friends decide how to spend Saturday afternoon. When a decision involves us, we want to express our ideas and give our input.

Tell us about a time when you helped make a group decision. You may have helped your parents decide whether or not to sign you up for dance or music lessons. Perhaps you helped make all the decisions required for a Christmas or birthday surprise. Right now, you and your parents may be deciding which sports programs are best for you, or what color to paint the house. It doesn't matter if the decision was big or small; we want to know how you felt and what you learned from the experience. The topic is, "When I Got to Share in Making a Decision."

Discussion Questions:

— What are the advantages of helping to make decisions that affect you?
— What do you usually contribute to the decision-making process?
— How do you feel when you are a part of the decision making process?

A Time I Had to Choose the Best of Two Bad Things
A Sharing Circle

Objectives:

The students will:
—weigh the relative consequences of difficult choices.
—apply universal moral values, such as honesty, respect and responsibility, as standards in decision making.

Introduce the Topic:

Have you ever been in a situation where you had to make a choice and it seemed like someone would get hurt no matter what you chose to do? Decisions like that are very difficult, but we all have to make them occasionally.

Maybe you had to choose between telling the truth and protecting a friend. If you told the truth, it would get your friend in trouble, but to protect your friend, you had to lie. Or maybe your mom asked if you liked the new clothes she bought for you. You didn't really like them or want to wear them, but you hated to hurt her feelings. Perhaps your family had to decide whether to allow a sick or injured pet to continue living — and suffering — or have it put to sleep. Have you ever done something you didn't really want to do rather than hurt a friend's feelings or risk losing a friendship? When both choices look bad, choosing seems like losing. And sometimes being honest is very tough. Think this over for a few moments. The topic is, "A Time I Had to Choose the Best of Two Bad Things."

Discussion Questions:

— How do you feel when you have to make a very difficult choice? What feelings do you have after you've decided?
— Can you think of an example where being honest is not a good idea?
— How does lying to others hurt you?
— How does doing the right thing, even when it's very tough, make you a better person?

A Time I Kept My Promise
A Sharing Circle

Objectives:

The students will:
—explain the value of keeping promises.
—associate feelings with honesty.
—associate honesty with the development of trust.

Introduce the Topic:

Today's topic is, "A Time I Kept My Promise." Have you ever made a promise to someone and kept it? You said that you were going to do something, or not do something, and you followed through — even though it might have taken some hard work. Maybe you promised your dad that you would sweep the kitchen or patio after school and you did it. Perhaps you made a promise to a friend that you would go to his house on a Saturday to help with math homework and you went, even though you had to give up a more enjoyable activity. Maybe you promised your teacher that you would try harder to be quiet during study time, and by really working at it you succeeded. Or perhaps you promised not to do something, like not to fight with your sister or brother when the two of you were alone. How did you feel about keeping your word? Did anyone notice or acknowledge you for keeping your promise? Try to remember a time that you made a promise and kept it, and get ready to share it with the group. The topic is, "A Time I Kept My Promise."

Discussion Questions:

— Why is it important to keep promises when we make them?
— How does it feel when someone makes a promise to you and keeps it? ...doesn't keep it?
— How does keeping, or not keeping, promises affect the willingness of others to trust you?

A Way in Which I'm Responsible
A Sharing Circle

Objectives:

The students will:
—describe responsible behaviors in which they regularly engage.
—discuss the benefits of choosing responsible over irresponsble behaviors.

Introduce the Topic:

The topic for today's circle is, "A Way in Which I'm Responsible." Think of a responsibility that you accept and carry out. It may be a chore that you do each week, like sweeping the kitchen floor or watering the lawn. Perhaps your responsibility is to do your homework every evening after dinner, or to read for a half-hour each night before bed. Maybe you get up on time every morning, or fix breakfast for yourself and your younger brothers or sisters. Do you earn and save money? That is a way of being responsible. Before we begin, think quietly for a few moments about something you do that is responsible. The topic is, "A Way in Which I'm Responsible."

Discussion Questions:

— What are some of the ways in which we are responsible?
— What did you learn by hearing about what other students do that is responsible?
— Why do you think it is important to be responsible?
— What can happen when you are not a responsible person?

We Cooperated to Get It Done
A Sharing Circle

Objectives:	The students will: —describe a situation in which a goal was met through teamwork. —describe the importance of cooperation in goal attainment.
Introduce the Topic:	*Today we're going to talk about teamwork and what it can accomplish. Our topic is, "We Cooperated to Get It Done."* *Think of a time when you worked with a group of people to get something done. You can talk about a team activity in which you've participated here in class, or some other cooperative group experience you've had. Perhaps you belong to a sports team that won a game, or a group of scouts that completed a big project. Maybe your family worked as a team to clean up the house or hold a garage sale. You and some friends may have done something together like cook a meal, plan a party, or hold a bake sale. Tell us what the group was trying to accomplish and how you felt being part of it. Take a few moments to think about it. The topic is, "We Cooperated to Get It Done."*
Discussion Questions:	— How did most of us feel about being part of a team? — Why is cooperation important when a group of people is working together? — What can happen if people don't cooperate? — How does working with a team on a school assignment affect the quality of your work? — How does it affect your attitude?

Something I Never Do When I Want to Make Friends

A Sharing Circle

Objectives:

The students will:
— express the need to belong.
— identify behaviors that can act as deterrents to friendship.

Introduce the Topic:

Making friends is kind of an art. There are things we can do that cause people to want to get to know us. And there are things we can do that are practically guaranteed to keep people away. Today, we're going to talk about the second group of behaviors — the roadblocks to friendship. Our topic is, "Something I Never Do When I Want to Make Friends."

What things do you purposely avoid doing if you like someone? Maybe you're careful not to be bossy or dominate conversations. Maybe you try not to be nosey, or make negative comments about what the person says or wears. Perhaps you've learned from experience that people are turned off by constant complaining or clowning around. Think about it for a few moments. The topic is, "Something I Never Do When I Want to Make Friends."

Discussion Questions:

— Why do you avoid the behavior you mentioned?
— Why is it important to know how to make friends?
— What are the benefits and risks of telling others about the things they do that turn us off?
— What can you do if you have trouble making friends and aren't sure why?

Additional Sharing Circle Topics

How I Help at School

How I Show That I'm a Good Citizen

How I Show Respect Toward Others

A Time I Helped Without Being Asked

A Promise That Was Hard to Keep

I Admitted That I Did It

I Stood Up for Something I Strongly Believe In

I Faced a Problem on My Own

I Told the Truth and Was Glad

I Kept an Agreement

A Responsible Habit I've Developed

A Time I Did Something to Help the Community

What I Wish I Could Do to Make This a Better World

People Seem to Respect Me When...

Someone Tried to Make Me Do Something I Didn't Want to Do

I Do My Best in School When...

A Time I Said "No" to Peer Pressure

A Way I Changed to Be a Better Friend

A Rule We Have in My Family

I Said Yes When I Wanted to Say No

A Time I Had the Courage of My Convictions

My Favorite Excuse

A Responsibility I Have at Home

A Time Someone Made a Promise to Me and Kept It

A Time I Didn't Keep My Promise

I Took a Positive Attitude Toward One of My Responsibilities

A Task I Didn't Like at First, But Do Like Now

An Irresponsible Habit I've Decided to Drop

A Responsible Habit I Plan to Have as an Adult

If your heart is in Social-Emotional
Learning, visit us online.

Come see us at:
www.InnerchoicePublishing.com

Our website gives you a look at all our other Social-
Emotional Learning-based books, free activities and
learning and teaching strategies.

INNERCHOICE Publishing

15079 Oak Chase Court
Wellington, FL 33414

CPSIA information can be obtained
at www.ICGtesting.com
Printed in the USA
BVHW061339100621
609274BV00008B/1381